Warmest wishes

Ruth Dorval Jones

by Lee McMillan

The Mary Lee McMillan Garden at the Woman's Club of Raleigh.

Mary Lee McMillan.

BEAUTIFUL NORTH CAROLINA AND THE WORLD OF FLOWERS

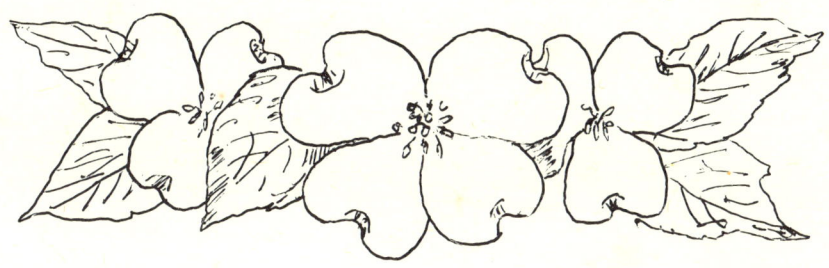

by Mary Lee McMillan and
                     Ruth Dorval Jones

MOORE PUBLISHING COMPANY — Durham, North Carolina

Copyright © 1979 by Moore Publishing Company, Durham, North Carolina.

Printed in the United States.

All rights reserved.

Library of Congress Catalog Card Number: 79-91037
ISBN: 0-87716-110-0

For information, write Moore Publishing Company, P. O. Box 3036, Durham, North Carolina 27705

Dedicated to Our Husbands

Robert Leroy McMillan
William Wright Jones

*Thy glory flames in every blade and leaf
To blind the eyes of grief
Thy vineyards and thine orchards bend with fruit
That sorrow may be mute.*

*A hectic splendor lights thy days to sleep
Ere the gray dusk may creep
Sober and sad along thy dusty ways
Like a lone nun who prays*

*Would in thy beauty, we might all forget
Dead days and old regret,
And through thy realm might fare us forth to roam
Having no thought of home—*

*October
— John Charles McNeill
Poet Laureate — North Carolina*

INTRODUCTION

We find it difficult to express our deep gratitude to the hundreds of members of the Garden Club of North Carolina and to the many nurserymen who have helped us in our endeavor and have left their mark on the state. The Garden Club itself is one of the most useful organizations in this state.

We must extend our thanks not only to these people but also to Mr. Herbert O'Keef, Mr. Paul Kelly and Mr. Clarence Steppe for their encouragement, and to Miss Nancy Darr of the White House Staff for her gracious support. And to the many contributors of articles in this book, once more, thank you.

Mary Lee McMillan
Ruth Dorval Jones

NOTES ON CONTRIBUTORS

Mrs. Ollie Adams — Chairman of the Landscape Restoration Committee of the Mordecai Plantation House in Raleigh.

Sally Buckner — English professor at Peace College in Raleigh and a former editor of the woman's page of the *Goldsboro Argus*.

Luther James Cooper — Past president of the Men's Garden Clubs of America and the American Hemerocallis Society.

Dr. C. C. Crittenden — Former head of the Department of Archives and History.

Frances Erdahl — The widow of the late Gerald Erdahl for whom the Cloyd-Erdahl Student Union Building at North Carolina State University is named.

Voit Gilmore — Well-known in North Carolina for his leadership in Boy Scout activities.

Gerald Johnson — Retired editor of *The Baltimore Sun* and a native of Riverton, North Carolina, located in Scotland County.

Paul Kelly — Formerly assistant director of the Department of Conservation and Development in North Carolina.

Nell Battle Lewis — Longtime Sunday columnist for the Raleigh *News and Observer*.

John Charles McNeill — A native of Riverton, North Carolina, and a former poet laureate for the state.

Frank Poole — A Raleigh physician.

Clarence Steppe — A landscape architect and owner of Wayside Nurseries.

Dr. B. W. Wells — Famous as North Carolina's first ecologist and also for his widely acclaimed book *The Natural Gardens of North Carolina*, published in 1932, Dr. Wells was once head of the Department of Botany at N. C. State University.

CONTENTS

Springtime in Beautiful North Carolina	3
My Garden	4
Sundials	6
Sunburnt Boys	8
The Lumbee River	9
The Ballad of Wisteria	10
The First "Ladies Garden Club" in the U.S.—1891	12
The Beginning	13
Raleigh: First Green Survival City in the U. S.	14
Raleigh Garden Club Firsts	16
Men's Horticultural Societies— 1804	18
Men's Garden Clubs of America	19
Ladybird Johnson's Beautification Program	10
John F. Kennedy Memorial	21
Some Public Gardens	22
A Sunken Garden (Balentine's)	24
The Story of WRAL-TV Gardens	25
Raleigh's Park Squares	26
The Marvin Johnson Gourd Museum	27
Southern Living Garden Show	30
Betty Smith's Walled Garden	31
Dr. Tom Daniel's Old World Garden	32
Ellen Mordecai's Garden—1830	33
Herbs	34
Button Gardens	36
The American Gardener—1804	37
Father of American Gardening—1771	38
The First American Landscape Architect	40
Martha Logan: First Garden Columnist—1752	41
A Royal Gardener	42
Rare Gardening Books (William Lanier Hunt Collection)	43
Cupola House—Edenton	45
Fairfield—Town of Lenoir	45
Four Oaks	45
Montmorenci Mansion	47
A Charming Map	48
Church Gardens	50

Laurel Hill Nurseries (Camellias)	51
The Camellia: History	52
The Sasanqua Camellia	53
Arranging the Camellia	54
The White House Baby and Willsforest Plantation	55
The Old Plantation: Richlands, Onslow County	56
The Jeweled Flowers of Salvador Dali (The Cheatham Collection)	57
The Cherokee Indian	58
The Cherokee Rose	59
The Raleigh Rose Garden	60
The Strange Story of the Peace Rose	61
The Christmas Rose	62
Bible Plants	63
Boxwood	64
The Cigarette Tree	65
Crape Myrtles	66
The Dogwood (State Flower of North Carolina)	67
Flowering Cherry Trees	68
Gardenias	69
Hemerocallis	70
Hibiscus (Rose of China)	71
Hyacinths	72
Lilacs	73
Lily of the Valley	74
Magnolias	75
Peonies	76
Poinsettias	77
Rhododendron	78
Smilax	79
The Coffee Tree	80
The Persimmon Tree	81
On Blueberry Hill with Katie and Bill McNally	82
Violets at Pity's Sake: Concord	82
My Mountain Home in Maggie Valley	83
North Carolina Trees in History and in Legend	85
North Carolina Parks	89
Wildflowers of North Carolina	95
Past Presidents of the Garden Clubs of North Carolina	98

Past Presidents of the North Carolina Federation of Woman's Clubs	99
Past Presidents of the Woman's Club of Raleigh	100
Past Presidents of the Raleigh Garden Club	101
Past Presidents of the Wake County Men's Garden Clubs	102
Past Presidents of the Raleigh Rose Society	103
Past Presidents of the North Carolina Camellia Society	103
Our First Ladies	105

BEAUTIFUL NORTH CAROLINA AND THE WORLD OF FLOWERS

A view in the garden of Mr. and Mrs. William Kemp of Goldsboro, N. C.

SPRINGTIME IN BEAUTIFUL NORTH CAROLINA

"The apple tree, the singing and the gold..."
— *Euripydes*

Around old hedgerows the wild plums with their fragrant snowy white blossoms bloom against the dark green scrub cedars and pines. About the middle of April they are white in the margins of woods.

The beautiful native crabapple with its small pinkish flowers has a delicate fragrance, and a cluster of it has the soft look of drifting fog.

The lovely river plums, shadblows, sourwoods, sparkleberries, hollies, silver bells, magenta and white redbuds, sweet bays and cherry laurels all grow in glorious profusion in North Carolina.

Flowering cherry, Japanese cherry, flowering plum, flowering apricot, flowering peach, crabapple, etc., are among the most decorative plants in cultivation, and all of them add to North Carolina's spring loveliness.

The double flowering peach with its white velvet petals is a great favorite with flower arrangers. The purple-leaved plum is one of the first to bloom. Most gardeners overlook the great beauty of the Tung oil tree, a native of China, which in spring is covered with charming pink and white flowers almost as large as those of the cotton plants.

Raleigh's Cameron Village with its myriad flowering crabapples attracts hundreds of visitors, and the North Carolina State College Memorial Tower, surrounded by flowering trees, has been described by someone as "frozen music."

Between the home of Mr. and Mrs. A. J. Fletcher and the Methodist Home for Children in Raleigh is a lane of flowering cherry trees. In the sunlight these snow white trees are a picture of shimmering radiance. They are just as lovely when the dew is on them as they are in cloudy weather, or when the rain is falling gently.

MY GARDEN

by Frank Poole

At intervals some bird from out the brakes
Starts into voice a moment, then is still
There seems a floating whisper from the hill—
 — George Gordon, Lord Byron

My friend Butch helped me build my greenhouse. When winter comes with its cold gray days and frosty nights it is here that I spend many pleasant hours starting new plants from seeds or from cuttings while enjoying the springtime color and fragrance of blooming flowers.

In February and March I go out into the garden and make ready to hang the sign that has gone up in April for the last eleven years just inside our rotunda flora holly hedge:

ALL VISITORS ARE WELCOME TO OUR GARDEN
HARRIET AND FRANK POOLE

Brick paths curve along the contours of the land, making our 175 x 145 foot lot seem much more spacious than it is. One cannot see very far down the path at any one place, creating the illusion that there is no end to the walkway. The paths split and meander along on both sides of the creek.

Dogwood trees shade the Coral Bell, Pink Coral, Snow, and Hundegeri azaleas and an occasional camellia and cucumber magnolia. Water recirculated from the creek spills from the small basin of our garden fountain down the hillside to a reflecting pool.

From here the path leads upward between this rippling stream and the dogwoods, trailing English ivy like Spanish moss, to our upper patio. Sitting there, looking out over the garden, we can hear the water cascading over the upper and lower dams in the creek. I always think of a line from Wordsworth:

"The cataracts blow their trumpets from the steep—"

Though the dams have mighty small trumpets, the sound of their waters spilling and splashing into the stream below is the kind of music that never tires my ears.

Another path leads downward through a mass of wildflowers, ferns, Jack-in-the-pulpits, trillium, Atamasco lilies and a bed of Indian mocassin.

Across an arched bridge there are more azaleas. These are the large ones—Formosa, Tabor White, and George L. Tabor, some of them ten feet tall. They surround a carpet of green grass that together with myriad hanging lamps gives the effect of a spacious outdoor living room.

It is in the upper patio, covered with a green awning for the summer, that we have our meals. Steps lead down to our favorite area, the big lower patio, which is surrounded by raised Charleston brick planters filled with Mother's Day azaleas and begonias and sultanas from the greenhouse. Twenty-five hanging baskets spill over with lacy ferns and bright-colored orchids and sultanas.

A beautiful, moss-covered, rough brick fountain and goldfish pool lulls us with the soft sound of falling water.

That our garden was designed, built, and maintained strictly by our family—Harriet, Jim, Bill, Cindy, and me—makes it a part of us and us of it.

Another reward from the daily care of sweeping the walks, pruning the shrubs, cutting the grass, and occasionally cleaning out the creek is the fact that I find myself in excellent physical shape. And this last task also offers a plus for the garden, as the creek loam is used in the front yard vegetable garden.

After the daily care for my patients is over I relax in my garden in the quiet of the evening with the song of birds, the croaking of frogs, the faint rustling of leaves and the sound of rippling water. I am lulled into daydreams of life and its meaning.

How, I wonder then, can sensible people live the life of alcohol, of permissive sex, of drug indulgence, surrounded by air and noise pollution? God's world can be found in all of us. Why can't they see it?

At the end of a long, hard, tiring day I find God's world in my garden. And it will still be there tomorrow and tomorrow and tomorrow.

SUNDIALS

With warning hand I mark Time's rapid flight
From Life's Glad Morning to its Solemn night
Yet, through the Dear God's Love I also show
There's Light above me, by the Shade below.
                         — John Greenleaf Whittier

Ben Eaton, a former member of Christ Church in Raleigh, is vicar of Littleham Church in Exmouth, England. Littleham Church was built in the twelfth century. A sundial dating back to the Norman period stands in the church yard, where the grave of Lady Nelson, wife of Lord Horatio Nelson, is also to be found.

"What a dead thing is a clock compared with the simple altar-like structure and silent heart language of the old sundial, the garden god of Christian gardens," Charles Lamb wrote.

" 'I will make the shadow cast by the declining sun on the dial of Ahaz turn back ten steps.' So the sun turned back the dial." And so even Isaiah referred to the sundial.

The earliest of all sundials of which we have proof was in Egypt about 1500 B.C. According to the position of the sun, the upright of the dial cast long or short shadows along a horizontal limb divided into six hours.

Another early type was the hemisphere of the Chaldean astronomer, Berosus, existant about 900 B.C. Centuries later the Greeks, with their more advanced theories of geometry, constructed dials of greater complexity, while the first sundial in Rome appeared in 290 B.C. Sundials were gradually improved, especially by the Arabs, and by the fourteenth century the day had been broken down into equal hours. The first striking clock was put up in Milan, Italy, about 1336.

A hundred years ago in English and American gardens, there were sundials almost without number. One bearing the date 1770 reads, "I stand among ye summer flowers, And tell ye passing of ye hours. When winter steals ye flowers away, I tell ye passing of their day."

Sir Walter Scott's sundial had the motto, "Night cometh."

Henry Van Dyke's sundial read, "Time is too slow for those

who wait; Too swift for those who fear; Too long for those who grieve; Too short for those who rejoice; But for those who love, Time is eternity."

Boxwood sundials can be found in Oxford and Cambridge universities today, and the very beautiful rose garden at the Morehead Planetarium in Chapel Hill has as its central focus a sundial that attracts many visitors.

SUNBURNT BOYS

by John Charles McNeill

Down on the Lumbee river
Where the eddies ripple cool,
Your boat, I know, glides stealthily
About some shady pool.
The summer's heats have lulled asleep
The fish-hawk's chattering noise,
And all the swamp lies hushed about
You sunburnt boys.

You see the minnow's waves that rock
The cradle lily leaves.
From a far field some farmer's song,
Singing among his sheaves,
Comes mellow to you where you sit
Each man with boatman's poise,
There, in the shimmering water lights,
You sunburnt boys.

I know your haunts; each gnarly bole
That guards the waterside,
Each tuft of flags and rushes where
The silver reptiles hide,
Each dimpling nook wherein the bass
His eager life employs
Until he dies—the captive of
You sunburnt boys.

You will not—will you?—soon forget
When I was one of you,
Nor love me less that time has borne
My craft to currents new;
Nor shall I ever cease to share
Your hardships and your joys,
Robust, rough-spoken, gentle-hearted
Sunburnt boys.

THE LUMBEE RIVER

by Gerald Johnson

An obscure little river, stealing through wide swamps in the low country of southeastern North Carolina has become one of the most celebrated streams in the state by the same process that made the Afton famous throughout the English-speaking world. A poet lived on the banks of the Lumbee and sang it into everlasting fame.

But the genius of John Charles McNeill was inspired by a beauty that is very real and very poetic. The river has none of the qualities that characterize other North Carolina streams—the immensity of the lower Cape Fear, the power of the Yadkin, the wild beauty of the Linville, the majesty of the Roanoke. Tranquility is the secret of the Lumbee's charm. It flows rather swiftly for a lowland stream, but only rarely is its dimpling surface broken by a ripple sharp enough to produce foam. Through an endless, winding colonnade of tall junipers, rosemary pines, and solemn, flat-topped cypress, it slips silently, shut off by green walls of almost jungle density from the wide fields of cotton and corn, the pine forests, and the picturesque homesteads of the plain sturdy folk who inhabit its valley.

Yet, prosaic as it seems to the stranger's eye, the cool, clear waters of the Lumbee, filtered by passage through miles of sandhills, but darkened by the stain of juniper roots, have in them something of the magic of those fabulous rivers of old of which it was said that he who tastes them once must ever strive to come to them again. Men have gone from its banks to all continents and over all the seas without forgetting its "shimmering water-lights," its "fish-hawk's chattering noise," and "the minnow's waves that rock the cradle lily leaves."

Always, sometime, somehow, it draws them back—and can more be said of Tiber?

THE BALLAD OF WISTERIA

by Gerald Johnson*

Yesterday the wisteria was almost in full bloom. Today it is in its glory. Tomorrow it will already have begun to fade. Among all the glories of the revolving seasons there is nothing more evanescent than this misty bloom that momentarily hangs like a cloud of purple incense around the house eaves and then disappears for another year.

The old Philosopher must have given his grave approval to the wisteria when, in the springtime, he raised his eyes from his archives in Chew, the state of Everywhere; for twenty-five centuries ago Lao Tze set down in his book of Reason and Virtue that to accomplish merit and acquire fame, then to withdraw, that is Heaven's Way.

Yes, certainly the man who hated ostentation above all things could have found no fault with the wisteria. There is nothing striking about it. It is as aristocratic as a Chinese gentleman who can trace his ancestry back for five thousand years. It thrusts its beauty upon no one. One gains from it no impression of happy friendliness such as bursts from the lowly dandelion, laughing impudently in the face of every passer-by; one gains from it no solace for a bruised spirit, such as the violet carries; least of all is it touched with the vivid passion of the rose.

Yet, it has a charm that is all its own, and one not inferior to that of any flower that blooms. It is the charm of quietness, the beauty of tranquility—the same that permeates the purple hazes of the twilights of autumn in the high hills. It is endowed not with the beauty of the hopes and loves and pleasures of our everyday life, but with the beauty of dream-stuff, too exquisitely fragile for a work-a-day world.

In every heart there are broken fragments of aspirations too high ever to be achieved, hopes too splendid ever to be realized, desires too mighty to be more than half understood, much less confessed. They are the wreckage of a dream world, purer, happier, and far more beautiful than the one in which we live.

*This was written by Mr. Johnson for the 1938-39 edition of the Garden Club Yearbook.

Under the hard necessities of existence we are compelled for the most part to ignore the existence of these ruins, for to do otherwise would be hopeless folly. Yet only the man who has succeeded in reducing himself nearer to the level of the brutes than the generality of mankind forgets them entirely.

And when the wisteria comes out, it throws for a few short days an enchanted veil over some wreck of a building, transforming it into a shrine where the old Philosopher might sit and meditate on things too high for habitation that he has built for this world, and might walk through the ruined city of his dreams.

Nor is it altogether a vain thing. For as he considers how fair were its palaces, how noble its colonnades, how its domes and turrets aspired to pierce the clouds, and as he then reflects on how lowly is the thing that he has actually done, he and the world will profit if he is moved to come back and add but a single stone to the structure that mankind is slowly raising toward Heaven.

THE FIRST "LADIES GARDEN CLUB" IN THE U.S.—1891

He shall be like a tree planted by the rivers of water that bringeth forth his fruit in his season; his leaf also shall not wither, and whatsoever he doeth shall prosper. For life is like a tree forever growing.

The twelve Athens, Georgia, women who gathered in the parlor of one of their flower-growing friends on a cold January afternoon in 1891 did not realize they were making gardening history.

Their little gathering marked the beginning of a movement that would spread across the entire country. It was the first meeting of the "Ladies Garden Club."

The twelve ladies were drawn together by a common interest in natural beauty and in the care of plants. They made a careful study of the earliest book on gardening in the English language, written by Thomas Hyll in 1568.

The Green Revolution and the Green Survival programs today are undoubtedly the result of the dedication of these women, who were inspired by the lovely ante-bellum homes with their elaborate gardens.

They did not realize that the Green Revolution and Green Survival would bring beauty to many people who love and appreciate the good earth.

THE BEGINNING

by Albert Coates
Professor Emeritus, Law School
University of North Carolina

Garden Clubs were organizing in localities throughout North Carolina before the 1900s. Individual women were trying to beautify the surroundings of their own homes, and this led to the efforts to beautify their neighborhoods, and then to beautify their communities.

On November 6, 1925, representatives from garden clubs in Asheville, High Point, Raleigh, Reidsville, and Winston-Salem met in Winston-Salem and organized the Garden Club of North Carolina. This state-wide organization now includes 800 local garden clubs with 18,000 members.

Mrs. Robert Leroy McMillan, a former president of the Garden Club of North Carolina, had this to say about its aims and purposes:

> Perhaps a careful study of the plan and program of the Garden Club of North Carolina from its organization will reveal one characteristic that belongs both to the club and to the state it represents—a silent but strong determination, little by little, to have this North Carolina that we love so much become the marvel that labor and love might make it. In our hearts we set no limits to what we think North Carolina might be. Formally and publicly we subscribe to our motto, *Esse Quam Videri*; but what I should like to write upon the portals of our state is the inscription from *The Fairie Queen*: 'All that in this delightful gardin growes, Should happie be, and have mortal bliss.'

RALEIGH: FIRST GREEN SURVIVAL CITY IN THE UNITED STATES

by Clarence Steppe

"Green Survival," as a philosophy, contends that the responsibility of protecting God's creation is an individual, personal obligation, and that when each of us does what each of us can do, the world will literally sing with beauty; and that is what the Bible says thousands of times.

> And out of the ground made the Lord God to grow every tree that is pleasant to the sight, and good for food ... And He took the man—whom he had formed—and put him into the garden of Eden to dress it and keep it.
> — *Genesis 2:8,9,15*

> And God said, Behold, I have given you every herb bearing seed, which is upon the face of all the earth, and every tree, in the which is the fruit of a tree yielding seed; to you it shall be for meat. And God saw everything that He had made, and, behold, it was very good.
> — *Genesis 1:19,31*

> When thou shalt besiege a city a long time, in making war against it to take it, thou shalt not destroy the trees thereof by forcing an axe against them: for thou mayest eat of them, and thou shalt not cut them down (for the tree of the field is man's life).
> — *Deuteronomy 10:19*

> And I brought you into a plentiful country, to eat the fruit thereof and the goodness thereof; but when ye entered, ye defiled my land, and made mine heritage an abomination.
> — *Jeremiah 2:7*

Now he that planteth and he that watereth are one: and every man shall receive his own reward according to his own labor.
— *I Corinthians 3:8*

Incline your ear, and come unto me... and I will make an everlasting covenant with you... For ye shall go out with joy, and be led forth with peace and the hills shall break forth before you into singing, and all the trees of the field shall clap their hands. Instead of the thorn shall come up the fir tree, and instead of the brier shall come up the myrtle tree.
— *Isaiah 55:3,12*

Thus saith the Lord of Israel — "Build ye houses and dwell in them, plant gardens and eat of the fruit of them."
— *Jeremiah 29:4-5*

And the Lord said unto me, Behold, I have put my words in thy mouth. See, I have this day set thee over the nations and over the kingdoms, to root out, and to pull down — and to plant.
— *Jeremiah 1:9,10*

RALEIGH GARDEN CLUB FIRSTS

*"Beauty is truth and truth beauty,"—that is all
Ye know on earth, and all ye need to know.*
— John Keats

"Nature has had a lavish hand in making this state lovely," said Mrs. Clyde Hoey, wife of the late Governor Hoey, when she opened the Radio Garden School of the Air of the Raleigh Garden Club on September 28, 1928. The aim of this school was to stress the importance of making North Carolina more beautiful by beautifying homes, roadsides, parks, filling stations, mountains and mansions.

In 1925 the Raleigh Garden Club was organized by the Civics Department of the Raleigh Woman's Club, under the chairmanship of Mrs. D. M. Hicks. The Garden Club has since either organized or promoted home and neighborhood development (Hands), anti-litterbugging, the first garden school in the United States in 1935, a state hospital chapel garden, dogwood and shade tree planting, the Model Mile, Blue Star Memorial Markers and Green Survival.

The official opening of the Garden Club's Dogwood Week in 1945 began with Governor Gregg Cherry planting a tree on the southeast side of Capitol Square. Later, in this same program, Governor Luther Hodges planted a tree on the north side of the Capitol grounds.

The Dogwood Committee of the Garden Club of North Carolina set as its goal the planting of one dogwood tree by every homeowner in the state.

The Model Mile Committee beautified the mile of U. S. Highway 64 leading into Raleigh.

The first Blue Star Marker in the state, a tribute to the armed forces who have defended the United States of America, was erected in 1949 by the Raleigh Garden Club. It is located on U. S. Highway 64 East, just at the site of the Wake County Memorial Hospital. This was given in honor of Mrs. R. N. Simms, the first Blue Star Marker chairman of the Garden Club of North Carolina, Inc., and a member of the Raleigh Garden Club.

Richardson Wright, editor of *House and Garden*, congratulated the Raleigh Garden Club for its superb Garden School, the first of its kind in the United States.

MEN'S HORTICULTURAL SOCIETIES — 1804

*The earth and common face of nature spake to me
Rememorable things.
The ghostly language of the ancient earth.*
— *Wordsworth*

The great London Horticultural Society, whose influence has been far reaching, came into being in 1804. The New York Horticultural Society was born in 1818, the Pennsylvania Society in 1827, the Massachusetts Horticultural Society in 1830 and the Charleston Horticultural Society a few years later.

At the first meeting of the Maryland Horticultural Society in 1833, Mr. John P. Kennedy described the object of every Horticultural Society as twofold: first, to explore and develop the useful properties of plants; and secondly, to supply the means of procuring and multiplying the rare and beautiful productions of nature.

George Washington was one of the first great horticultural authorities in the New World. He was indefatigable in planting seeds and nuts sent to him from different parts of the country, and distinguished men of every country have listed horticulture as one of their greatest pleasures in life.

Mr. Sam L. Fairchild of Reidsville was elected president of the Men's Garden Clubs of America in 1970. He said, "Thirty-eight years ago stalwart men joined together in national unity to meet and discuss the problems and joys of gardening...

"We today must broaden our gardening horizons. We must not only teach those around us the techniques and mechanics of how to grow better plants, how to produce more crops on less land, how to grow plants in unsuitable environments; but we must teach them to correct attitudes and frames of mind, and educate our people to a proper use of their leisure time."

MEN'S GARDEN CLUBS OF AMERICA

by James L. Cooper

With about 12,000 members, Men's Garden Clubs have helped to plan and landscape many parks, interstate highways and public and industrial buildings. Through gardening awards they have stimulated a desire for beauty within our cities.

Local clubs have good meetings and present programs of special interest to local groups. The national organization offers many booklets and pamphlets regarding gardening topics. The local groups work with both the local and federal governments to help prevent additional pollution and clear up present pollution. They sponsor many youth gardening programs in schools and housing projects and encourage young gardeners to raise vegetables and flowers. They also help with Green Survival programs.

Men's Garden Clubs are always ready to work with local groups in any community project. They work with state and federal groups to save endangered species of wildflowers and shrubs. They help to remove and preserve species which might be destroyed by new private and public developments. Anyone interested in this kind of program can get in touch with the national or local Men's Garden Clubs for more information.

The Raleigh Men's Garden Club puts on a spectacular display of flowers each year at the North Carolina State Fair in Raleigh.

LADYBIRD JOHNSON'S BEAUTIFICATION PROGRAM

What does he plant who plants a tree?
He plants a home to heaven anigh,
For song and mother-croon of birds
In hushed and happy twilight heard.

— Bunner

President Lyndon Johnson said, "I want to make sure that the America we see from our major highways is a beautiful America. The planned program is not designed merely to beautify the highway but is to preserve and enhance America's countryside as well. Driving for pleasure is America's number one form of outdoor recreation. What you see of America is what you see from your car." President Johnson asked that high priority be given to landscape projects for screening junkyards, excavation scars, and other unsightly areas.

Mrs. Lyndon Johnson spearheaded a national beautification program which led to the organization of state groups throughout the country. Mrs. John D. Robinson, of Wallace and Raleigh, was appointed by Governor Dan K. Moore to be executive director of a program which sought "the logical and orderly development of the resources of the state."

Mrs. Robinson subscribed to her minister-father's motto, "The selfish person is an unhappy person." In 1968, as a result of her efforts, some 850,000 elementary school children were involved in the North Carolina Pilot program. Some 350,000 high school students were expected to participate the following fall.

The beautification program involved, among other things, cleaning up schools and school grounds, planting and seeding, and offering adult classes in landscaping.

Ladybird Johnson wrote to Mrs. McMillan, "It is the President's hope that community leaders and businessmen, ladies clubs and school children throughout the United States will look anew at their immediate surroundings and undertake those many small deeds of enhancement which can lend grace and joy to our lives."

"Kit" Steppe, ambassador of Green Survival, recently stated:

> No person in our generation has remotely approached the motivation of the greatest of gardeners, Mrs. Lyndon B. Johnson. She was not only a First Lady, but also America's leading gardener.
>
> In appreciation for the magnificent job she accomplished, many citizens and nurserymen are contributing plants and money to the Lyndon B. Johnson Memorial Grove, Washington, D. C., as a sign of their respect for the late President, but also as a token of their affection for Ladybird.

JOHN F. KENNEDY MEMORIAL

And thou, Oh God, by whom are seen
Thy creatures as they be,
Forgive me if too close I lean
My human heart on thee.
        — John Greenleaf Whittier

In the Green Room of the White House hangs a beautiful Monet flower painting, a memorial to our late, martyred President, John F. Kennedy. A portrait of John James Audobon, by John Syme, and the exquisite "Nocturne," by James McNeill Whistler also hang in the room, complementing the Monet.

Flowers are sent almost daily from the White House greenhouses to the tomb of John Kennedy as well as to the tombs of other Presidents and national heroes.

SOME PUBLIC GARDENS

There are hundreds of parks in North Carolina, many in use the year round. And each region of the state has several lovely gardens. They vary from the mid-eighteenth century gardens of Tryon Palace in New Bern* to the Airlie Gardens in Wilmington with their blend of the formal with natural vegetation.

Among these gardens, the magnificent North Carolina Botanical Garden at Chapel Hill covers over 300 acres of pine and deciduous woodlands, fields and streams. There visitors may enjoy a variety of wildlife and many species of native plants. Public trails are open daily.

The Elizabethan Garden, created and maintained by the Garden Club of North Carolina, is located on Roanoke Island, near Manteo and adjacent to the Lost Colony site and historic Fort Raleigh. The Garden Club, with the cooperation of the state of North Carolina, has created a lasting contribution to the culture of the state and nation.

The Woman's Club of Raleigh is the site of the Mary Lee McMillan Garden, landscaped and planted by the distinguished Lewis Clark and Clarence Steppe. It was presented to the Woman's Club by the Raleigh Garden Club and friends.

The Martha Franck Fragrance Garden at the Rehabilitation Center for the Blind in Butner is another notable garden, one of the first of its kind in the country. Clarendon Gardens at Pinehurst, featuring a large collection of hollies and flowering shrubs, cover approximately twenty acres. Greenfield Gardens, located in Wilmington, are beautiful with an abundance of azaleas, camellias, native ferns, and wildflowers.

Among the larger garden spots are the Biltmore Gardens, located in mountainous Asheville, which cover thousands of acres of shrubs and trees, together with beautiful formal gardens featuring boxwood, azaleas, rhododendrons, and other native flowers. Airlie Gardens in Wilmington are lush with flowering shrubs, camellias, azaleas, wisteria, evergreens, and other native North Carolina treasures. Orton Plantation at Wilmington is not

---

*The late Mrs. J. E. Latham gave generously of her energy and resources to promote Tryon Palace gardens. The dedicated efforts of Miss Gertrude Carraway and Mrs. J. S. Michener have continued this great tradition.

only a magnificent example of the old Southern Plantation but is also landscaped beautifully.

North Carolina has given encouragement to thousands of garden lovers, among them Mr. and Mrs. Robert Holmes of Mount Olive, Mr. and Mrs. William Rand of Garner, Mr. and Mrs. William Kemp of Goldsboro, Mr. and Mrs. Les Marbury of Wilmington, Mr. and Mrs. J. C. Osborne of Smithfield, and Mr. and Mrs. Carl Holleman of Apex. Jim Cooper's garden in Raleigh is a mecca for hemerocallis lovers.

A SUNKEN GARDEN
(Balentine's)

... a source of inspiration and renewed confidence in the goodness of our Creator...

Mr. Red Balentine has created a small sunken garden just outside his Cameron Village restaurant. This simple area of brick paving with its rich collection of indigenous plants and the sound of the flowing water there create truly a gem of timeless beauty.

It is a quiet and pleasant garden. Visitors usually forget that the area was once a space 80 by 30 feet, with the restaurant window looking across to a parking deck, the whole being depressed about sixteen feet below street level.

The area is dominated by the rooflike branches of an extremely large crape myrtle. Local bamboo varieties provide a curtain through which the garden is viewed. Camellia sasanquas are used as a background for a sheet of water continuously falling into a pool enhanced by "feather rock." The bamboos, with their tall stems, feathery foliage and slender, arching trunks add much to the overall beauty of the garden.

Dr. Lewis Clarke, a landscape architect, and Mr. Clarence M. Steppe, a nurseryman, the men who designed the gardens, installed an atomized mist system among the plants to provide the high humidity needed.

It is rare for nature to be thus reinstated. Mr. Balentine's garden is an inspiration to all businesses.

THE STORY OF WRAL-TV GARDENS

In 1958 when WRAL-TV moved its television station to its present address on Western Boulevard in Raleigh, the tract of land consisted of approximately four and one-half acres. The owner of the property and television station, A. J. Fletcher, decided to make a garden spot of three acres. He retained some of the pines and dogwoods and with the planting of thousands of azaleas and other shrubs, slowly developed the sides of the basin leading down to a fountain in the level area surrounded by a large lawn. There are winding flagstone walkways and permanent cement benches among the trees and shrubs.

The gardens are used for many different functions: garden parties, outdoor concerts, outdoor opera performances, band concerts, and weddings.

In addition to many individual visitors, there are guided tours by garden clubs. school classes and other organized groups. Students and teachers in the horticultural department of N. C. State University use the gardens for classroom purposes. In addition to several thousand azaleas, there are various other shrubs and plants, including lilacs, quince, American red bud, smoke tree, snowball, golden chain, camellia, hibiscus, rhododendron, lucidum, red leaf maple, hydrangea, and many others. The lawn is Kentucky fescue. In season, the following bedding plants are used: pansies, coleus, tulips, caladia, marigolds, begonias, salvia, and red geraniums.

Mr. Fletcher was presented a national award by the American Association of Nurserymen for the landscaping and maintenance of the gardens.

RALEIGH'S PARK SQUARES

In 330 B.C. when Alexander the Great conquered the last of the great Persian monarchs, he found the Persian gardens so incredibly beautiful that he cherished and cultivated them. The Greek historians, Diodorus and Shibo, described the loveliness of the ancient gardens so vividly that landscape men can reproduce them today.

Perhaps the Raleigh fathers were thinking of these beautiful gardens when in 1792 they laid out the plans for the city to include four park squares.

Caswell Square was named for Richard Caswell, the first governor of the independent state of North Carolina in 1776. It is now occupied by the state health office building. Burke Square was named for Governor Thomas Burke, elected in 1781. Burke also helped to frame the North Carolina state Constitution and formed Article II of the Articles of Confederation. Burke Square is now the site of the Governor's Mansion.

Only two of the original squares are left for "park sitting" and the brass bands which are no more. Nash Square was named for Abner Nash, who was elected governor in 1780. Moore Square was named for Alfred Moore, Associate Justice of the U. S. Supreme Court. A soldier, he saw action at Moore's Creek Bridge near Wilmington, an action which historians claim turned the tide of the Revolutionary War in favor of the Americans. Because of the dedicated efforts of the Raleigh Parks and Recreation Commission these two squares remain as lovely parts of Raleigh.

THE MARVIN JOHNSON GOURD MUSEUM

by Sally Buckner*

Peace of mind comes out of the harmony of life.

At Kennebec, the Marvin Johnson estate located off highway 55 on the outskirts of Angier, North Carolina, is housed the Marvin Johnson Gourd Museum. Surrounding it are forests, goldfish ponds, gourd plantings, a sparkling twelve acre lake and Mary Johnson's wildflower garden.

Americans tend to think of gourds in terms of long-handled, honey-colored dippers filled with cool, fresh well water at Grandpa's farm. In a modern affluent society, one might expect gourds to become as passé as homemade soap from a lard kettle. However, the specimens on exhibit at this museum demonstrate the versatility and usefulness of this common plant. In the hands of a creative workman it may become a musical instrument, household utensil, toy, or a work of art, as beautiful and up-to-date as Danish crystal.

Hundreds of visitors come each year to see the spectacular display of gourds lining the shelves. Most of the gourds were raised by Marvin Johnson himself and decorated by some of the gourd enthusiasts with whom he corresponds regularly. Some specimens retain their original shape and coloration but are transformed into works of art by skilled carvers, such as Theo Shoon of New Zealand, or Dr. Leslie Miller of Ohio. Shoon is a professional artist, who for a period of time worked with the Maori tribe, whose custom is to bury a hand-carved gourd with the body of a loved one. Some of the designs he uses date back to 1300 and take up to three weeks to complete.

The shape of some gourds dictates their use and decoration. . . . Small egg-shaped specimens are halved, jeweled, beribboned, lined and sometimes outfitted with miniature scenes, like the finest decorated Easter eggs. Globe-shaped pieces are frequently used as hanging lamps. Some of these have holes drilled in intricate patterns and shine like star constellations when the light is turned on.

*This article was included in *A Traveler's Guide to North American Gardens.*

Many of the specimens in Johnson's museum are composite pieces, combining parts and wholes of differently shaped gourds. Only in such fashion could one get elephants, cats, teapots, teacups, eagles, roosters, camels, dolls, pioneers, Puritans, Santa Clauses, shepherds, madonnas. Some of these are left in their natural color, but many are beautifully painted. One elephant is a brilliant turquoise accented with gold. A large teapot has an enameled blue bowl, a red handle, lid, and spout, and gold accents. One teacup from Argentina has a sterling silver rim and "sipper."* A bottle from Africa is completely covered with beads.

One particular display that is dear to Marvin Johnson's heart is a miniature locomotive engine, formed entirely of gourds. It is a replica of the Number Three engine Johnson's father used to run on his logging operation.

Some of the most interesting pieces use the inside of what is popularly known as the "dishrag" gourd. This variety has a comparatively thin outer husk and a stringy inside not unlike the plastic mesh balls purchased in supermarkets today. Pioneers used that inside material as dishcloths. During World War II, it was also used as oil filters. Current craftsmen have molded the stuff into dolls (similar to the dolls fashioned from corn husks), or fashioned it into lacy lampshades.

Although most of the items in Johnson's museum were grown right on his farm, some have come from as far away as Ecuador, Peru, Africa and even China. The latter country is represented by a cricket cage made from ivory teak, and one small gourd. Along a far wall is one display consisting entirely of musical instruments made from gourds. There is a "thumb-piano," a gourd to which is attached a series of metal strips; flipped with the thumb, each strip sounds a different value of the musical scale. The marimba looks something like a curved xylophone; its wooden "keys" are struck with a wooden hammer, and the gourds beneath act as sounding boards to mellow the tone. One large sitar features intricate ivory inlays. From Mexico come colorfully enameled maracas.

*According to Mary Johnson, this is a maté teacup, used to serve tea made from the leaves of a yerba mate tree. The tea is sipped through a sterling "bombilla," much like a straw. The serving of this tea gives the message, "You are welcome in this house."

A number of specimens have historical significance. In the nineteenth century, small bottle-shaped gourds were used as shot and/or powder containers. One such powder container in Johnson's collection is unusually flat; Johnson believes that it was so molded as it grew against a rail fence. On it are etched several sets of initials and the date 1840. Johnson has another gourd, an exceptionally large bowl, which was planted in 1883 by Sarah Suzanne Price near Chimney Rock, North Carolina. He also has a snapshot of Miss Price's niece, Eugenia Price McKenzie, as a baby, seated inside; her aunt's gourd served as precursor of today's molded plastic babyseat, no doubt. Another display of historical interest features paper money from Haiti, which country, according to Johnson, in 1860 paid off its debts with gourds, then valued at twenty cents apiece. From that date, the Haiti bill has been termed the "gourde," just as our bill is referred to as a dollar.

SOUTHERN LIVING GARDEN SHOW

In the miracle of spring what greater delight is there than to behold the earth appareled with plants as with a robe of embroidered work set with Orient pearls.
— Gerard

The feature attraction at a Southern Living Garden Show held in the Merchandise Mart in Charlotte, North Carolina, was a floral clock, almost thirty-six feet in circumference and made entirely of cacti. The clock kept perfect time. It was surrounded by huge asbestos planters, each containing large specimens of cacti. This clock was modelled after the famous floral clock in Edinburgh, Scotland, always a source of great interest to tourists.

The show was spectacular, with landscape gardens bursting with blooms and foliage, flower shows with more than fifty artistic arrangements, special exhibits and table settings. There were handicrafted items that ranged from rare polished stones to intricate wood carvings and exquisite hand embroideries.

Also featured were home and room settings and a gardener's market place with African violets, azaleas, camellias, cacti, and calla lilies for sale.

At least eighteen hundred blooms were used. Daffodils, hyacinths and tulips produced early and colorful bloom for the show.

No international flower show could be more beautiful than this. In addition, this show was of special value to Southerners because it featured plants designed for this section of the country.

A second magnificent Southern Living Flower Show was one which featured Cloud Nine Dogwoods, indescribably lovely against a background of Canadian hemlocks and white birch trees, set amid trailing arbutus, purple violets and fern and mosses.

Water trickled under a bridge on a trail made of Crab Orchard stone bordered with low walls of pink and other stone from Jacobs Creek Stone near Mount Gilead, North Carolina.

BETTY SMITH'S WALLED GARDEN

Some little old melody would sweep our heart strings, and send through us the sweetness of love and tenderness, the swift passing, cloud-like of forgotten faces, the echoes of voices now forever still, the pensive tinge of kinds of happiness nevermore possible, the fragrance of strange lilies blowing in the twilight casements of the past.

— *Dr. Frank Crane*

The profits from her best selling novel, *A Tree Grows in Brooklyn*, enabled Betty Smith to buy the 150-year-old "Old Mangum Place" in Chapel Hill, with its two acres of lawn and many magnificent century-old oak trees. She had always dreamed of a walled garden, and there she created one with her own hands, to be enjoyed especially on cold, wintry days. Over the mantel in her living room hung a large painting of her childhood home in Brooklyn.

"It is beautiful to me," she said, "because it represents my childhood and children seem to have a way of making life beautiful. Just to live is wonderful. I love life and I love children."

She also had a large painting of her Brooklyn ailanthus tree hanging in her living room, and outside her front door she planted a redbud tree in memory of that other tree.

Mrs. Smith said, "That old tree made possible all the beauty of this home and garden which we enjoy so much in Chapel Hill.

"This Tree of Heaven," she said, "drops seeds. No matter where a seed falls it makes a tree which struggles to reach the sky."

DR. TOM DANIEL'S OLD WORLD GARDEN

A garden is the greatest refreshment to the spirits of man.
—*Francis Bacon*

According to its picturesque history, the Franklinia (*Gordonia Altahama*) was discovered by John and William Bartram in a small area on the Altahama River in Georgia, in 1765.

The tree was first named Franklinia after Benjamin Franklin. It is thought that all plants available today were offshoots of the specimen in the Bartram Gardens near Philadelphia, Pennsylvania.

This rare tree (or shrub) has a five-petalled white flower, cup-shaped and centered with pale gold stamens.

Dr. and Mrs. Tom Daniel are fortunate to have this seldom seen shrub in their old world garden on Sussex Road in Raleigh.

The foundation of the garden's wall, as well as the enclosing walls, the old brick acorns and pineapples (age old symbols of hospitality), the pineapple chandeliers and waxed brick floors were made by Dr. Daniel himself. The old bricks, which he collected from dismantled plantation houses, have the names of their makers on them—Worthington, Bullard, Bryant, Jones, Davis, and Watson.

ELLEN MORDECAI'S GARDEN—1830

by Mrs. Ollie Adams

The silver dews of night are softly falling,
The stars are on the heather.
— Murdock McLean

In 1830, Ellen Mordecai was ten years old. In her book, *Gleanings from Long Ago*, she tells about this period of her life spent on Mordecai Plantation in Raleigh.

"A favorite place for us to play was the garden. It was a big, old-fashioned garden with walks running at right angles, laying off the beds. There were borders for flowers, separated by planks from the vegetable part, and on these borders grew old-fashioned flowers, white lilies, cups and saucers, butter-and-eggs, violets, poppies, fragrant white violets. I never saw blue violets until years afterward.

"Sister Margaret, Emily, and I played there on pretty days, summer and winter. The wheelbarrow house in one corner, which was a little shed just high enough for the wheelbarrow, was a great place for a house.

"We each had a house. One was the wheelbarrow house, one the yellow jessamine and lilac bush (the yellow jessamine climbed on the lilac bush) and I don't remember where the third house was.

"Then there were all the herbs. Rosemary—it was the custom in old English times to put a sprig of it in the hands of the dead as a symbol of the Resurrection. When Brother Jack died, years after, we put a sprig of rosemary in his hand.

"Aunt Harriet Lane often brought home wildflowers and plants from her excursions into the woods. She planted a 'Grandsire Graybeard' (Fringe Tree) and other trees on the place.

"Plant nurseries were rare then and neighbors exchanged cuttings of plants and plants themselves. Some of the Mordecai roses were called by the names of the persons who had given them to us. We had the Becky Casso rose and the Conk rose. We also had the cabbage rose, Monthly Damask, and cinnamon rose."

HERBS

by Frances Erdahl

Herbs, with their scented leaves, seeds, and roots, reward the gardener in his search for fragrance.

When "in fourteen hundred and ninety-two, Columbus sailed the ocean blue," he was not searching for new lands. He sought the spices of the Indies. That he changed the course of history was incidental.

Herbs were so highly prized in the Dark Ages that they found careful cultivation—and sanctuary—in the monasteries. Monks of the Benedictine and Cistercian orders cultivated them for condiments and medicines.

Four hundred years before the birth of Christ, Theophrastus, a pupil of Aristotle, studied about these same herbs and wrote about them. And cummin is mentioned in Isaiah and in Matthew as a portion of the tithes paid by the Pharisees in Judea.

Herbs were brought to America by the early settlers and were used in old family remedies and in flavoring. They were used when storing the linen and were strewn on floors and burned for fragrance. Some helped to disguise the taste of old meat; some were used to dye homespun fabrics, and some were used as love potions or witches' brews.

Modern interest in herbs centers in their culinary uses and in their use in cosmetics, perfumes and potpourri. Camomile tea is a favorite tonic for weak stomachs and is also used in almost every beauty parlor in the United States for rinsing blond hair. Laurel, or sweet bay oil, has been used for insect stings for generations. Lemon balm, basil, borage, burnet, chervil, chives, sweet cicily, cress, dill, oregano, parsley, pennyroyal, sage, summer savory, shallots, rosemary, tarragon and thyme are herbs most frequently used in the kitchen.

The following herbs can be grown in winter if their environment is cool and light: basil, dittany, lemon verbena, parsley, rosemary, sweet marjoram, tarragon and perhaps peppermint.

Mrs. Willis Reid of Raleigh has one notable local herb garden, fifty feet square and bordered with grass paths and brick edging.

Yard-wide brick paths extend from the corners to a circular path in the center.

At another spot is an old stump holding a tall piece of weathered wood. In this circle are many of Mrs. Reid's favorite herbs, including tray sage, lemon balm, bee balm and lamb's ear. The outside circle is bordered with germander. Narrow paths cut through and make triangles. In each triangle a different variety of mint grows. Low-growing herbs are planted in the front beds and taller ones in the back.

Mrs. Reid and Mrs. Clyde Patton are famous for their "Tussie Mussies" (small nosegays) made from herbs. They use:

        Viburnums
        Daphnes
        Lemon Verbena
        Geranium foliage
        Lamb's ear
        Fringed gentians
        Miniature roses
        Violets
        Grape hyacinths
        Anemones

BUTTON GARDENS

All about me were the rejoicing looks of flowers, and the shining hush and loveliness of dew-hung ferns and bushes, and the gentle, pure passion of the sunlight.
  — *Archibald Rutledge*

This woodland scene is re-created in the tiny button garden. Its fairy beauty brings a breath of the outdoors to invalids and shut-ins.

The base of each tiny garden is a button, preferably a large one. On the button base place such things as tiny figurines, shells, bits of glass, pebbles, colored sand, seed pearls, bits of coral, bits of hand-carved ivory or sandalwood fans, jade and ivory filigree, pearl belt buckles, sequins, bits of mica, seeds, pods and the smallest available fresh, dried or artificial flowers.

A tiny forget-me-not or violet looks almost like a dahlia in a button garden. Small succulents and cacti provide a growing element. The wax rose family, with its tiny rosettes of silvery, pinkish green, makes an exquisite addition.

These little gardens do not require soil though some people put a pinch of sand or peat moss in the center. If given a drop of water every day with a medicine dropper they will stay fresh a long time.

The little objects are glued into place with transparent glue. If a plastic bottle cap is glued to the bottom of the button and filled with water, the dainty flowers can be inserted in the holes of the buttons and will reach the water.

Mrs. John Farrior and Mrs. Daisy Scott of Raleigh have made hundreds of these chaming little gardens for hospital patients.

THE AMERICAN GARDENER—1804

Awake, oh North Wind, and come thou South
Blow upon my garden that the spice thereof may flow out.
  —Song of Solomon

The Reverend Mr. Robert Sutton, an Episcopal minister in Pittsboro and grandfather of Mrs. Alex Badger of Raleigh, was the owner of a copy of *The American Gardener*, written in 1804 by John Gardiner and David Hepburn. The list of other owners of this volume includes some illustrious names: Thomas Jefferson, five of his cabinet members and thirty-five Congressmen, Aaron Burr and James Madison, having two copies.

General John Macon, as Jefferson a subscriber for three copies, described David Hepburn as "a worthy and honest man, well skilled in all the various branches of gardening, not to be excelled as a practical man in the cultivation of vegetables and fruit trees."

Hepburn's gardening instructions included such phrases as: "soil riddled free of lumps," "should hoar frost seize the plants," "a situation which enjoys the sun," "whisk off the earth with a light broom," and "rough cast the seed."

The book described herbs used as medicines, pot herbs and sweet herbs. For example, it described cardoons—related to artichokes—which were used in cooking and in curdling milk to make cheese. Elecampane and rocambole, medicinal plants, were used in treating pulmonary diseases. "Skirrets" had white, sweetish roots which were edible.

FATHER OF AMERICAN GARDENING—1771

Jefferson's services for liberty are immortal. Wherever men look out of darkened windows of despotic governments they are cheered by the light of Jefferson's Declaration, which penetrates and illumines the deepest cell of tyranny.... In any decade of the World's history the words and deeds of Thomas Jefferson are like a bow of promise set in the heavens.
— *Josephus Daniels*
Secretary of the Navy, World War II

"I heard a nightingale today."

Thus wrote Thomas Jefferson in 1787 while making a tour of Europe.

As early as 1771 Jefferson had begun making entries in his notebook about the development of his beloved Monticello in Virginia. He spoke of his garden as a "canvas at large, to be grove, of the largest trees, poplar, oak, elm, maple, ash, hickory, chestnut, Scotch broom, calycanthus, althea, gelder rose, magnolia, glauca, azalea, a fringe tree, dogwood, redbud, wild crab, kalmia, mexeren, eunonymous, halensia, rhododendron, oleander, service tree, lilac, honeysuckle and brambles."

In 1808 Jefferson wrote, "I know of no source of amusement and health equal to botany and natural history." His botanical library became in time one of the best in America, and the beautiful serpentine brick walls of many Virginia gardens were designed by Jefferson.

As the result of his interest, the State of Virginia in 1818 appropriated $15,000 to be devoted to the building, equipment and manning of a state university. He provided that botany should be taught there. For the university botanical garden he proposed "exotics of distinguished usefulness and accomodated to our climate."

His *Notes on Virginia*, published in 1782, represented the first important contribution by Jefferson to biological science and served as a landmark in his career. The chapter dealing with the flora of Virginia gives lists of medicinal, esculent, ornamental and otherwise useful plants.

In his lifetime, Jefferson was governor of Virginia, ambassador to France and twice President of the United States. He was instrumental in the United States' purchase of the Louisiana Territory in 1803, and because of his enthusiasm the Lewis and Clark Expedition was formed and sent out. In writing the epitaph for his tombstone, however, he wished to be remembered only as the champion of freedom of thought as the author of the Declaration of Independence, the author of the statute of Virginia for Religious Freedom, and as the father of the University of Virginia, a place where men could be taught to think for themselves.

A man of many facets, Jefferson's feeling for flowers was expressed in these words: "The flowers come forth like the belles of the day. The hyacinths and tulips are off the stage, the irises are giving place to the Belladonnas, as these will do to the tuberoses."

THE FIRST AMERICAN LANDSCAPE ARCHITECT

"Leave now the homestead and the old stone wall—"

Andrew Jackson Downing* was America's first great landscape architect. His *Treatise on the Theory and Practice of Landscape Gardening* affected the trend of gardening in this country and inspired the next great American landscape architect, Frederick Olmstead, who laid out New York's Central Park, the grounds of our national Capitol, and other great American parks.

Downing's work was familiar to William Ashe, who left his home in Raleigh to become a United States forester. He offers an example of how man can remake the green face of the earth through the exchange of plants by sending many rare specimens to his sister, the late Mrs. George Flint, also of Raleigh.

Mrs. Flint especially prized a pink locust tree. Brother Will had also sent her a gingko tree. According to Mrs. Flint, "[The ginko] has leaves like a giant maiden hair fern. Its autumn coloring is wonderful. It is one of the oldest trees in the world and is sacred in India and China."

However, North Carolina itself is outstanding in its flora. According to Ashe, the state has more varieties of trees than all of Europe.

---

*Andrew Downing is mentioned in *Dragonwyck,* the best-selling novel by Anya Seton. Nicholas Van Ryn, the patroon of the estate is said to have been influenced by Downing in laying out its grounds.

MARTHA LOGAN
First Garden Columnist — 1752

Fair flowers, bright waterfalls and angel's wings.
— *Edgar Allan Poe*

A fascinating widow, Martha Daniel Logan, of South Carolina, is said to have been the first garden columnist in the United States. In 1752 the *South Carolina Gazette* carried her "Garden Kalendar." In 1779 it was reprinted in the *Palladium of Knowledge*.

Though she started a nursery business in 1753, Mrs. Logan was also adept at truck farming. An instance in her "Gardener's Kalendar" suggested planting oranges "in the change of the moon" and root vegetables "in the full of the moon."

Mrs. Logan carried on a "seed correspondence" with John Bartram of Philadelphia, the American botanist to King George III of England. Bartram established the first botanical garden in America at Kingsessing, Pennsylvania. Mrs. Logan not only exchanged bags of seed with Bartram but also sent him olives, indigo, passion flowers, oleanders and other plants in ships that sailed from Charleston to Philadelphia.

A ROYAL GARDENER

Unlike Old King Cole, his nursery rhyme counterpart, King George III was not "a merry old soul." With all his faults, however, this king, who reigned from 1760 to 1820, did love flowers. He supplied the British Royal Society with the *Endeavor*, a ship which sailed around the world for three long years in search of new plants.

Joseph Banks, a young man of great wealth and a member of the Royal Society, was given permission to sail on this ship. He took with him grain, vegetable and flower seeds to use in trade with the natives of each place the ship docked. On this expedition he secured the services of the famous Swedish botanist, Dr. Solander, and also two artists.

When Banks returned with many plants and animals, including flax from New Zealand and the kangaroo of Australia, he was welcomed at London with great acclaim by the king and other important people. Banks later helped in the settlement of Australia and is known and honored there as "the Father of Australia." Because of his endeavors he was knighted by the king and later made Royal Adviser at London's Kew Gardens.

During the reign of King George III more than seven thousand plants were brought to England, most of them through the efforts of Sir Joseph Banks. Banks was responsible for sending the famous botanist, Robert Brown, to Australia to collect plants and seeds which would later be grown in Kew Gardens. It was largely through his efforts that King George III's Kew Gardens are world famous for choice flowers of surpassing beauty.

Just as the Kew Gardens were the projects of Sir Joseph Banks, the Edinburgh Gardens in Scotland, established during the seventeenth century, owe their beauty to George Forrest. In telling of one of his dangerous plant exploration trips in Tibet, Forrest recalled being chased by a party of lamas. He was shot at with poisoned arrows, and by the end of the chase his feet were so swollen that he could hardly walk. Just the same, he got his plants.

In his career Forrest was responsible for collecting more than thirty thousand plants. The Edinburgh Gardens contain these as well as many valuable hybrids.

RARE GARDENING BOOKS
(William Lanier Hunt Collection)

In the dim and distant past the magic of flowers was recorded on the walls of temples.

Some time ago the University of North Carolina exhibited in its Wilson Library rare gardening books and exquisite flower prints from the library of William Lanier Hunt of Chapel Hill, nationally known landscape artist and writer.

"Gerard's great *Herbal* (1597), which has kept coming out in new editions, is often called the most fascinating book ever published on plants," Mr. Hunt has commented. "The lovely little North Carolina wildflower, Gerardia, was named for Gerard.

"It is hard to believe that any book written in 1629 could be interesting to gardeners in 1974, but John Parkinson's book (1629) is probably the most interesting book on gardening in existence today.

"John Parkinson was both apothecary and herbalist to King James I, which means that he was druggist and botanist. His six-hundred-page book is better than anything we have today. Opposite each page of printed matter is a beautiful woodcut showing the plants he is writing about.

"The title, *Parkinson's Paradisi in Sole*, is a play on words. In the seventeenth century "paradise" meant park or enclosed garden and so the title is a play on the author's name, Park in sun.

"Southern gardens are full of the old flowers mentioned by Parkinson. He said, '[Violets] are the spring's chief flowers for beauty, smell and use,' and 'French marigolds have a strong, heady scent, both single and double, whose glorious show of color would cause many to believe there were some rare goodness or virtue in them.'

"John Rea's garden books include engravings of American plants. 'In three books and in so many Beds,' John Rea said (1665), 'I have lodged earth's beauties.'

"John and Jane Loudon grew three thousand species and varieties of plants in their small garden in Bayswater, a suburb of London, besides editing and writing books. Mrs. Loudon's books were written for women with small homes. Her flower plates are exquisite. Her books are invaluable today to Southern gardeners.

"Camellia growers will be interested in seeing the first really accurate drawings of a camellia in the rare work by Kaempfer (1712), one of the most fascinating travel books of any century. Kaempfer went to the Orient in 1683 and made beautiful and accurate drawings of the plants he saw in Persia, Russia, India, Japan, etc.

"In these books some of the woodcuts and illustrations are so carefully done that any gardener can distinguish one variety from another almost as well as in the color plates of modern catalogues."

Mr. Hunt has expressed the hope that someday these horticultural treasures might be reprinted so that nature-loving gardeners can own them.

Mr. Hunt is a fellow of the Royal Horticultural Society of England, a native of North Carolina and a specialist in the horticultural problems of the South. His library deals largely with plants from parts of the world with climate similar to that of the southern United States.

The highlight of the exhibit was Plukenet's *Opera Omnia Botanica*, which was published in sections between 1692 and 1705. The steel engravings in it are considered the finest of their kind, and among them are some of the earliest engravings of American plants. This copy of the *Opera* was originally owned by Daniel Solander, a favorite pupil of Linnaeus, and a botanist on Captain Cook's voyage to the South Seas. Mr. Hunt feels certain that the book accompanied Solander on the *Endeavor* in 1768. The appearance of the book indicates that it has been taken to sea.

Other books on exhibit were *Paxton's Magazine of Botany* (1834) and Ellen Willmott's folio volumes of *The Genus Rosea*, issued in parts between 1910 and 1914 and illustrated in color by Alfred Parsons.

CUPOLA HOUSE—Edenton

The Cupola House in Edenton, North Carolina, was built in 1758 by Francis Corbin, the haughty land agent of Lord Granville, the Lord Proprietor and owner of half of the province of North Carolina.

The last owner of the house, Miss Tillie Bond, sold the interior of the eighteenth century parlor to the Brooklyn Museum, and the Cupola House now has a replica of the original room.

FAIRFIELD—Town of Lenoir

Fairfield was built by James Harper in 1825. Harper was postmaster at Fairfield from 1840 to 1865. His cancellation stamp was carved from holly, and this unique heirloom is now in the possession of the British Museum.

FOUR OAKS

He restoreth my soul.
— Psalm 23

Mr. and Mrs. Joe Austin of Four Oaks bought the beautiful wrought iron fence which used to enclose the Cameron Mansion on Hillsborough Street in Raleigh. The fence now encloses their Four Oaks garden, which is filled with camellias, azaleas, magnolias, bulbs and other lovely flowers.

Mr. Austin says of the garden, "Many of my most pleasant hours are spent grafting camellias. . . . There is nothing better for mind and spirit than to go into the little greenhouse on a freezing January or February morning and see fine camellias at their peak of bloom."

The original stairwell of Montmorenci Mansion. It is now part of the Winterthur Museum in Wilmington, Delaware.

MONTMORENCI MANSION

The romance of old places speaks with gentle voice and without the jarring notes of tragedy. In harmony with the high traditions of a great past, I summon the people of this state to arise to meet the responsibility of making this a more beautiful state.
— *Governor Clyde Hoey, 1938*

More than a quarter of a century ago, Montmorenci Mansion, the famous house built around 1822 by General William Williams at Shocco Springs, near Warrenton, North Carolina, was sold at auction at the county courthouse door to the highest bidder for $850.

The highest bidder was Miss Elizabeth Thompson, pioneer interior decorator of Raleigh. She had the house dismantled, and a few months later the DuPonts of Wilmington, Delaware, bought the house for their Wintherthur Museum.

Mr. John A. H. Sweeney, curator of the museum, says that the graceful, free-hanging stairway which dominates the stair hall in the Winterthur Museum was formerly the outstanding feature of Montmorenci. "The staircase," he commented, "was probably constructed by a North Carolina craftsman, but whether it was designed by a professional architect is not known."

The stairway resembles the elliptical stairs illustrated in Peter Nicholson's, *The Carpenter's New Guide*, a builder's handbook first published in London in 1792 and widely used in America during the first half of the nineteenth century. Gouge carving and finely molded plaster work suggest the refined taste of the Federal period.

The dado and trim found in the elegant Baltimore Room of Winterthur, cocoa in color, are from Montmorenci. Mr. Sweeney thanked Miss Thompson publicly for saving Montmorenci, agreeing with one appreciative visitor who called the mansion "architectural poetry."

A CHARMING MAP

by Nell Battle Lewis

"Ours is a land like that promised Israel!" the late Governor Angus W. McLean once exclaimed in a burst of patriotic hyperbole. Though even the staunchest patriot must admit that that is putting it a little strongly, it is true that naturally North Carolina is a rich and beautiful land, in many ways favored by a generous heaven.

The organization most interested in the natural beauties of this state is the Garden Club of North Carolina, and a charming expression of that interest is a pictorial map of the state, nineteen by thirty-four inches, which the Garden Club has just had printed in eight colors by the Winston Printing Company of Winston-Salem. It was designed by Mable Pugh, head of the Art Department of Peace Junior College. Mrs. R. L. McMillan, President of the Garden Club of North Carolina, was chairman of the map committee, and Mrs. H. H. Totten, of Chapel Hill, president of the state club when the map was designed, will manage its distribution.

Maps have always had a peculiar fascination for me, and from this one I derive special pleasure. On a yellow background it shows pictures of some of the most interesting of the more than three thousand varieties of flowering plants that grow in this state, in the localities where they are found. Down in the southeast, for instance, the unique insectivorous Venus' fly-trap is depicted, and in Harnett County, the rare Sandhill Pixie. Laurel and rhododendron, trailing arbutus and galax, decorate the mountains. The peach orchards of Moore County are a bright pink, and the cotton country in the east is indicated by white blooms of that plant. On the mainland across from Roanoke Island the mother of all the scuppernong vines is memorialized with a cluster of grapes.

Trees are shown as examples of certain varieties found in the state, pines and live oaks, redbuds and dogwoods. Statesville is marked by the large-leaved magnolia.

Note: This article first appeared in the Raleigh *News and Observer* on July 18, 1937.

A few buildings are depicted, too: the Capitol, of course; St. Thomas Church in Bath, the oldest [church] in the state; the great Gothic cathedral that tobacco built at Duke University; the Mint Museum in Charlotte; the houses in which Dolly Madison, Andrew Jackson, and James K. Polk were born; The Grove, Willie Jones' home in Halifax; and the towers of the old market house in Fayetteville and old St. Paul's Church in Edenton.

Towns that have organized garden clubs are marked by a red flower. Several well-known gardens are noted: the iris garden at Duke, those at Airlee and Orton on the Cape Fear, the Arboretum at Chapel Hill, the Biltmore gardens near Asheville and the ivy gardens near Junaluska. A red jug indicates the Jugtown Potteries and a blue jug those around Smithfield. Two toys mark Tryon.

Several full-rigged ships sail the bright blue sea to the east, and under one of them just off Nag's Head is the name, Theodosia Burr [the daughter of Aaron Burr, lost at sea in a storm off the coast]. The big compass without which no pictorial map is complete and which on this map is painted red, blue and yellow, has for its center a dogwood blossom. Surrounding the map is a decorative border showing in alternation, North Carolina birds and wildflowers, twelve varieties of each. On what otherwise would be a blank South Carolina are the seals of the State of North Carolina, of the Garden Club of North Carolina, and of the national Council of State Garden Clubs Federations against a spray of long leaf pine and yellow jasmine. The state flag is in the upper left-hand corner.

This map is a beauty. I shall speedily frame a copy of it and hang it conspicuously in my house.

CHURCH GARDENS

As the garden causeth the things that are sewn to spring forth...

Flowers have ever been part of the radiant beauty of holiness when man communes with his God. To monastery gardens, medieval cathedral gardens and Oriental temple gardens we owe much of the floral knowledge that has come down to us through the centuries.

The National Cathedral Garden in Washington is a mecca for all gardeners. In North Carolina there are many church gardens: Siler City, Bailey, Charlotte, Fayetteville, Goldsboro, etc.

Mrs. William Kemp of Goldsboro has designed and planted an exquisite garden of camellias, azaleas, pansies, white daffodils, white hyacinths and white tulips for the Episcopal Church of Goldsboro.

She has commented that the garden "has become a big part of our church life. We use it for gatherings of all sorts, even bridal receptions.... I like to see strangers rest awhile before going on their way. People who have loved ones in our local hospital sometimes go to our little garden for peace and quiet and inspiration."

Mrs. David Oates of Fayetteville has said, "In the old days most country churches had big lawns with fine old trees, yards suitable for picnics, homecomings and other affairs, with a minimum of foundation planting. A few especially old city churches would have a small garden with brick walls, boxwood, a garden ornament, an old bench or a concrete seat.

"At Holy Trinity Episcopal Church we have a camellia memorial garden with a beautiful entrance gate of old brick and wrought iron. In the center of the garden is a handsome lead fountain. Our sasanquas, camellias and azaleas are so filled with blossoms that the flowers are often used in our altar vases in the chancel, in the children's chapel, and for the ill and shut-ins. There is a handsome hedge of Cleopatra Sasanquas between the church and the rectory grounds."

LAUREL HILL NURSERIES
(Camellias)

A little way within the fragrant dewy forest where giant yellow pines, full of dim contralto music, rejoiced in the sunshine—just here I heard a warbler singing high over the dreamy waters of a woodland lake.
— *Archibald Rutledge*

In 1950 Mr. J. S. Howard was brought to his paternal home in Salemburg, a sick, bedridden man, unable to walk. In his pain he made a compact with God that if he were spared he would make the world more beautiful for others.

Today his camellia trail winds along a mill pond with over 1,000 varieties of camellia plants ten to twenty-five feet tall. There is a section devoted to the Betty Sheffield family of camellias and another to the Tomorrows, with a pink and a white part. Howard's Laurel Lake Gardens have long been a mecca for flower lovers. Azaleas and hollies grow in profusion under the tall pines.

Mr. Howard has said, "Camellias saved my life and all I want now is to leave something here for people to enjoy."

Mr. Howard donated a set of the lovely Betty Sheffields for the National Arboretum. He has done much to encourage the National Camellia Society and is most active in the largest of the local camellia groups. His habit has been to donate a plant to each new member of the local society, and he has donated plants to gain new members in Wilmington, Fayetteville, Baltimore, Washington, Norfolk and other communities. In 1977 alone he was responsible for 110 new members for camellia societies.

THE CAMELLIA: History

*High in the heavenly blue this chorister was,
Joyous in that halcyon repose that the heart
Enjoys when it is at peace.*
                      — *Archibald Rutledge*

"Celestial raiment of an angel" is the name the Chinese give the Camellia Magnoliaflora, and the camellia has a history worldwide which complements this description of the flower.

The camellia is a native of Japan and China. Rich brocades, vases and screen prints from the East often display camellia designs. Large camellia trees more than 300 years old grow in a temple courtyard near Kunming, China.

In 1639 Kamel, a Moravian Jesuit, presented the Spanish queen with a glossy plant bearing white flowers. The radiant blooms pleased the king so much that he ordered the flower planted in the royal greenhouses. In 1735 Linnaeus, the eighteenth century's foremost botanist, named the lovely flower for Kamel.

The camellia figured in the mysteries written by the late Agatha Christie. She chose the camellia as the emblem of her favorite brain child, Hercule Poirot, the incomparable detective who was featured in so much of her writing.

"It would have to be a camellia," she said. "It is so immaculately clean and tidy, like himself. Glossy and elegant. It couldn't be anything else."

In 1797 John Stevens, of Hoboken, New Jersey, imported the single red camellia japonica from England. Three years later Michael Floy brought the Alba Plena from Devonshire, England. Today America is the leading camellia grower of the world. President Andrew Jackson, at an affair of state, adorned the White House, lit with wood fires and candles, with tiers of camellias and larentia, and President and Mrs. Franklin Pierce, at their State dinners, always presented the lady guests with a camellia corsage.

THE SASANQUA CAMELLIA

*Thy plants are . . . a fountain of gardens,
a wall of living waters, and streams from Lebanon.*
— *Song of Solomon*

The first news that reached Europe of the wonderful flowers of China came as decorations on ancient porcelains. Beautiful camellias were pictured on tall vases and jars, and over the years many gardeners have succumbed to the ineffable loveliness and charm of the sasanqua camellia in particular. A hedge of tall-growing, semi-double pink sasanquas is a thing of rare beauty. Mr. and Mrs. William Rand, of Garner, are local gardeners famous for their planting of sasanquas, a magnificent sight when in full bloom.

John Harris, the Tar Heel Gardener, says of it: "It is a flowering evergreen that blooms at a time in autumn when there is little else blooming. What it lacks in flower size and quality is compensated for by the number of blooms.

"It is the only flowering evergreen that will tolerate a great deal of sun and heat without extra watering. It is easily seeded, rooted or layered."

ARRANGING THE CAMELLIA

"Yet another year of hope and promise in our world of flowers...."

Camellias floating in a silver or crystal bowl have an airy loveliness. Yet the Orientals believe that the radiant beauty of this flower can only be displayed by using the whole branch. Whichever way is chosen, the camellia is a flower which lends itself to arranging.

Camellias are perfect for use in the Byzantine spire arrangement, for example. For this arrangement a water-soaked oasis cone should be anchored in an epergne, urn or chalice and the flowers placed in it symetrically. One very beautiful spire made entirely of camellias uses deep rose-colored ones at the bottom, delicate pink in the center section and white ones at the top.

One table decoration so stunning that it was used for several years at the annual reception of the North Carolina Society for the Preservation of Antiquities consisted of a forest of fifteen or twenty ceramic Christmas trees. They were painted with white satin glaze, and each tree had many tiny white plastic lights. The trees were placed on a long mirror reflector, festooned with garlands of Southern smilax and white camellias.

THE WHITE HOUSE BABY
AND WILLSFOREST PLANTATION

I bring fresh showers for the thirsting flowers
From the seas and from the streams;
I bear light shade for the leaves when laid
In their noonday dreams.
— *Shelley*

In one of the three famous "holly houses" on Tilden Street in Raleigh—now the home of Bessie Buck—lived Anne Howe Cothran, niece of President Woodrow Wilson, and Perrin Cothran, a State College professor. At President Wilson's insistence their baby was born in the White House and was known the world over as the "White House baby."

This house, built several decades ago by Mr. and Mrs. H. C. Evans, is on the high ground just before the deep cut of the Norfolk Southern Railroad. The holly tree has a circumference of over 105 inches, just short of nine feet.

A second notable holly house was Willsforest, the Greek revival mansion of Major and Mrs. John Devereaux, which was removed many years ago to make way for the railroad. It was built in 1840 by Ann Willis Lane Mordecai, widow of Moses Mordecai, and her daughter, Margaret Mordecai, who married Major John Devereaux. Their descendents believe the holly tree was planted by Mrs. Mordecai, who started many fine trees, shrubs and flowers.

The name Willsforest was derived from that of a favorite slave, Will, who lived in the forest near the knoll selected as the site of the magnificent brick house. The mansion was distinguished not only by the holly but also by the portico with its immense white fluted columns topped with graceful Ionic capitals and by the library's extensive collection of rare books.

The third of the great hollies grows on the grounds of what was the Stephenson home, the parental home of Mrs. William Yoder.

THE OLD PLANTATION
Richlands, Onslow County

*How often in dreams I tread a path
Where the ox-eye daisies grow
Or gaze through the night from a farmhouse door
At the heavens with stars aglow,
To hear, in fancy, again, the brook
That sings in the old ravine.
And nothing in life can compensate
For the loss of that cherished scene.*

"The Old Plantation," written by James Battle Averitt, in 1901, describes Richlands: "It is situated in the old county of Onslow, named for Sir Arthur Onslow.... [Its] broad, fertile acreage [is] embellished here and there with the largest hickory trees the writer has ever seen....

"The plantation proper is almost as level as a parlor floor, save where one beautiful stream cut through the fields as it went on its way with sparkling waters to the river.... Let us stand there a moment or two and take in the outline of the house. You see, it is a very large house.

"Yes, inclusive of the piazzas, it is just 60 feet square, three stories high, built of the best North Carolina pine and weatherboarded with fine yellow poplar. The house is of wood, but of such woods as the modern house builder never finds in these days. It is the very best of the original forests, carefully selected and seasoned."

This is the homeplace of Mrs. B. C. Kesler of Raleigh. Mrs. Kesler says of it, "Richlands is so named because of the rich and fertile soil. At my old home we have hundreds of fine old bulbs, many century-old boxwoods, old azaleas and enormous camellias. We have many old roses, too."

THE JEWELED FLOWERS OF SALVADOR DALI
(The Cheatham Collection)

> *I think of science as walking to and fro in God's garden, busying itself with its forms of beauty, its fruits and flowers, its beasts and birds and creeping things, the crystals shut in its stones and the gold grains of its sands, and coming now at length in the cool of the long day upon God Himself, walking in His garden.*
> — *Dr. W. L. Poteat*

Salvador Dali, whose magnificent jeweled flowers were purchased by the Cheatham Foundation in 1958, said, "In the period of the Renaissance great artists did not restrict themselves to a single medium. Leonardo da Vinci's genius soared far beyond the confines of a picture. His scientific spirit envisaged the possibility of miracles under the sea and in the air—new realities.

"Cellini, Botticelli, da Lucca created gems for chalices and goblets—jewelled ornaments of puissant beauty."

One of Salvador Dali's jeweled flowers is called "Living Flower." In it two golden flowers rise on gold stems from a malachite base. The top blossom remains in full bloom while the bottom blossom opens and closes electrically. It contains 1,381 diamonds.

Another jewel in the Owen Cheatham collection is called "The Light of Christ." This is so powerful that it disintegrates the cross, signifying the conviction that no evil can withstand the power of Christ.

"The Madonna of the Aquamarine" is, according to Dali, an aquamarine tabernacle resting in the gold medal of the Madonna. Her halo is circled with diamonds.

THE CHEROKEE INDIAN

Many things Nokomis taught him—
Showed the Death-Dance of the Spirits,
Warriors with their plumes and war-clubs,
Flaring far away to northward
In the frosty nights of winter:
Showed the broad white road in heaven,
Pathway of the ghosts, the shadows,
Running straight across the heavens,
Crowded with the ghosts, the shadows.
— From "The Song of Hiawatha"
Henry Wadsworth Longfellow

The bas relief carving of a stalk of corn, a symbol of immortality, on the front door of the hospital at Cherokee moved Mrs. Franklin D. Roosevelt to exclaim: "I have never seen anything more beautiful." The wife of another President, Mrs. Benjamin Harrison, was so impressed by this symbol of eternal life that she incorporated Indian corn and goldenrod when painting a china service for the White House.

"The Indians realize that their great knowledge of the world about them is something that cannot be learned except in the Book of Nature," Mrs. Tom Hines says. Her father, Dr. Clyde M. Blair, was superintendent of the Cherokee Indian Reservation in North Carolina.

"Many of the Indians are artists with a great dignity in their achievements. They have found a gain in the work itself, not outside it. They believe with Robert Henri, 'Art when really understood is the province of every human being. It is simply a question of doing things well.'"

Charlotte Hilton Green, author of *Birds of the South* and *Trees of the South*, comments: "After the discovery of America many new foods developed by the Indians were introduced to the world. Some of these were potatoes, tomatoes, corn, pumpkin, many kinds of beans, chocolate and vanilla."

THE CHEROKEE ROSE

The desert shall rejoice and blossom like the rose.
— *Isaiah*

The Indians regard all flowers as conscious, friendly beings whose beauty is a reflection of love and whose petals bring healing. One flower in particular, the Cherokee rose, traditionally offers the message that all Indians should remain together under the pine fringes of the forest and that no foreigner can inflict on them a sorrow which they cannot bear.

The belief exists that the Indian maiden who wears Cherokee roses in her hair will be happy throughout her life. One legend of the Cherokee Indians tells that during the Revolutionary War their most beautiful maiden carried a bouquet of the lovely flowers to the tent of a wounded American soldier whom she loved. Today the white Cherokee rose is the official flower of the state of Georgia. The pink Cherokee rose with its enormous single flowers and golden stamens is also deserving of the reputation accorded it in Indian legend.

Geological records show that roses predate man by millions of years and may have come into existence as much as seventy million years ago. Six centuries before the birth of Christ, the poetess Sappho glorified the rose as the queen of flowers.

Visitors to the old Andrew Johnson house once located in Pullen Park in Raleigh were enchanted by the profusion of Cherokee roses which covered its fence. This rose also abounds at the old Riverton home of John Charles McNeill, North Carolina's beloved poet. It has a history of being used for arrangements which began long before florists brought the floral treasures of the world to us as a matter of course.

THE RALEIGH ROSE GARDEN

When the perfume of the rose enchants us and we daydream of towering old rose sweetness, of exquisite rose gardens, of a split rail fence with a dazzling display of roses, we are following the ancient tradition that links the beauty of the spiritual life with the beauty of the rose.

I walked among my roses wet with dew
Alone one lovely morn.
Alone, I thought, but soon I knew
God also walks at dawn.

It is spring again.
I stand underneath the tree gazing upward,
feeling its green and gold beauty.
It showers down its yellow button flowers
Cascading in arches of golden gems from top to bottom.
It is a union of strength and weakness, effort and time.

As each tiny petal is gently wafted downward by the breeze
It promises me it will return.
God always re-creates beauty, someplace, somewhere, sometime.
— Virginia Norton

In 1937 the Raleigh Rose Society conceived the idea of the Raleigh Rose Garden, to be planted in the bowl of an old automobile speedway. Today this garden is the only accredited municipal rose garden in North Carolina. There are thirty beds in a formal design, containing in all some eighteen hundred rose plants. Each year the garden receives the new A. A. R. A. award winners. Mr. Charles B. Huyett and Mr. Frank Evans of the Raleigh Parks and Recreation Commission have charge of this garden. The Raleigh Rose Society works with the Parks Division in a consulting capacity.

THE STRANGE STORY OF THE PEACE ROSE

Only the nightingale understands the rose.
— Indian lore

Mary holding the Rosa Mystica; Mary in rose gardens; Mary crowned with roses; Mary accompanied by roses in her miraculous appearances at Guadelupe, Fatima and Lipa: So have artists depicted the rose. By the thirteenth century the rose had become one of the most important Christian symbols. It signified the Holy Trinity, Christ's crown of thorns, Christ's wounds, and the joy of redemption, as well as the Virgin Mary. Perhaps the earliest painting of a rose (Rosa Gallica) is one found in a Minoan fresco painted in Crete about 1500 B.C.

There is something mystical about the Peace rose in particular, considered by many rosarians the most beautiful rose of the century. Its shades of color vary from flower to flower through the changing seasons. M. Meilland, the great French rose hybridizer, called the Peace rose a rare discovery of the kind which occurs only once in a century.

Still unnamed after a breeding program begun in 1935, budwood was smuggled out of France in 1939—the year war broke out—in the diplomatic pouch of the American consul of Lyons. It reached the Conrad Pyle firm in America on the day Germany threatened to sink any U. S. ship which entered the war zone.

Finally, this, the world's greatest rose, was named for the world's greatest desire, peace. It was christened at the Pasadena Rose Show on the day Berlin fell in 1945. On V-E Day delegates to the United Nations Conference in San Francisco found Peace roses in their rooms, presented by the American Rose Society.

THE CHRISTMAS ROSE
(Holy Night Rose, Rose of Noel, Christ's Bloom)

This rose is said to have been created by the angel Gabriel for an impoverished shepherd girl, Madelon, who had followed the shepherds to the manger in Bethlehem. As she stood weeping, God pitied her and sent the angel Gabriel to comfort her.
"Why do you weep?" he asked.
"Because I have nothing to give to the babe and his mother."
The angel touched the frozen ground with his staff and there appeared the lovely blossoms of the Christmas rose. Madelon picked these and took them to the infant Jesus.

The white and unchallengeable flawlessness of the Christmas rose (Helleborus Niger) will reward any grower who takes the time to understand its simple requirements. Many growers advise that the roses like to be left undisturbed from year to year. Planted in an appropriate area and according to the vigor of the plant and the subsequent care given it, the rose will establish itself quickly. It cannot tolerate strong wind and grows best in half shade with good drainage and a soil that never dries out completely. A topping of leaf mold in autumn and in spring acts as a protective mulch for the plant. The pure white flowers with their clusters of gold stamens, green nectaries and stigmas in the center are things of beauty blooming in midwinter. One clump may produce forty to fifty flowers each year, and many growers such as Mrs. Jack Riley of Raleigh have made the Christmas rose an important part of their rose gardens.

BIBLE PLANTS

*Is thy soft pipe still ringing
Oh, lonely shephard boy?
What song art thou singing
In thy youth and joy?*

— Landon

Travellers to the Holy Land often speak of the cool beauty of the garden at Bethany. Against the darkening sky one may see the white doves and the two thousand-year-old olive trees and sometimes hear a shepherd pipe a lonely call.

More than a quarter of a century ago the New York Botanical Garden issued a descriptive list of over 150 herbs, trees, shrubs and flowers of the Bible, along with their generic names and the scriptural verses referring to them. About that time the International New York Flower Show featured a garden which included all the Biblical plants available then. It was a horticultural display occasioning great interest.

The plants referred to in the Bible in many cases were probably different than we conceive them to be. For example when Jesus spoke to the multitude near the Plain of Gennasaret, the "lilies of the field" to which he referred were probably the brilliant anemones—windflowers—which grew in profusion there. The humble dandelion was probably the "first fire of spring."

The pink flax is another plant of the Holy Land, blooming in Palestine in the spring, filling the land with its fragrant beauty, and for centuries supplying linen for clothing. Noah made his ark from the cedar growing there, and it is said that the aloe tree came to us from a stick carried by Adam from the Garden of Eden.

Many plants grown in Biblical times are grown in Southern gardens today, among them the cotton which Southerners see as uniquely theirs.

BOXWOOD

*The glory of Lebanon shall come unto thee,
the fir tree, the pine tree, and the box together,
to beautify the place of my sanctuary, and
I will make the place of my feet glorious.*
— *Isaiah 60:13*

Boxwood is a symbol of eternal life, and it can trace its ancestry back between 500,000 and 1,500,000 years. Since the days of the Roman supremacy it has been considered the best of all plants for hedges, and during the reign of Louis XIV it was grown in the lavish Versailles gardens.

Box cuttings were brought from the "old country" by the earliest settlers. There was the lovely Tuckahoe plantation with its box maze. When George Mason, author of Virginia's Declaration of Rights, built Gunston Hall he planted his great "box allée," said to be the oldest in Virginia. At Stratford, built about 1725, Thomas Lee found enjoyment in the elegant simplicity of the box-shadowed walks.

Some gardeners advise that boxwood does not seem to mind red clay soil, while others say the plants prefer friable, fertile soil generously supplied with organic matter, peat moss, leaf mold, etc. They do require good drainage and also a great deal of water. Sprigs six or eight inches will put out roots. Pine needles can be used as mulch. Mrs. Richard G. Stone, wife of the former president of St. Mary's College, had a large rooting bed, and many of the lovely boxwood gardens throughout the state are the recipients of her generosity and skill.

Dwarf boxwood is one type which is special in that it should not be pruned but allowed to grow freely. The plants get wavy or billowy on top and are at their prettiest when covered with their new growth in the early spring.

THE CIGARETTE TREE

On a summer day in the month of May
A burly bum came hiking
Down a shady lane through the sugar cane
He was looking for his liking
As he strolled along he sang a song
Of the land of milk and honey
Where a bum can stay for many a day
And he won't need any money.
Chorus
Oh! The buzzing of the bees in the cigarette trees
At the soda water fountain
At the lemonade spring where the blue bird sings
In that big rock candy mountain.

The cigarette tree, also called the Indian Bean tree, is really a catalpa. This tree is a favorite with fishermen because its light green, heart-shaped leaves seem to provide the food most sought after by the big, black caterpillars fishermen use for bait.

The flowers, appearing in the spring, are about 1½ inches long, white with purple dots and two rows of yellow dots in the center, and they are fragrant and borne in long panicles. The slender, cylindrical seed pods are about a foot long and are called Indian beans or cigarettes.

The catalpa's durable wood is used for fence posts among other things. Fishermen have planted many fast-growing catalpa trees to provide breeding places for their home-grown fishing worms.

And on hot summer nights all over the country, guitar and banjo players sing the old North Carolina folk song—about the cigarette tree and the big rock candy mountain.

CRAPE MYRTLES

The South should be one of the very lovely lands of the world.

— *Sherwood Anderson*

According to the late Dr. Clarence Poe, publisher of the *Progressive Farmer*, the Japanese called the crape myrtle "the flower of one hundred and one days" because it bloomed so long and so profusely. The tree is a native of China although it also thrives in India; in the south of England; in Europe, where it was introduced in 1759; and in southern areas of the United States. The oldest botanic garden in the world, located in Padua, Italy, boasts crape myrtles twenty-five feet high.

Crape myrtles which have been carefully tended by five different familias have been preserved in the Quail Corners Shopping Center in Raleigh. These magnificent trees now grace the streets at this shopping area on the Falls of Neuse and Millbrook Roads.

There are other beautiful plantings of crape myrtle in North Carolina. The approach to "Longview," home of Dr. Clarence Poe, was lined with crape myrtles "beautiful enough for a king's palace." Another North Carolina garden, designed by Mr. S. W. Buchanan, features powder blue salvia, blue and violet petunias and hemerocallis with dwarf white and Near East crape myrtles, whose giant trusses of bright light pink flowers often grow as big as waste paper baskets.

Our great President Andrew Jackson had so many crape myrtles they cast a rosy glow over the whole garden.

THE DOGWOOD
(State Flower of North Carolina)

He works with God for all posterity
Who spades the earth to plant a dogwood tree.

Springtime in this northern hemisphere means awakening. Gray, velvety buds, the shade of pewter, miraculously turn into green bracts, and the green bracts into the ethereal beauty of clouds of white dogwood.

With their red berries and foliage, dogwood trees are equally spectacular in autumn. Even in winter their bare branches make lacy shadow patterns against the gray skies.

Folklore tells us that dogwood furnished the timber for the cross and that Jesus in His mercy gave the tree forever after a slender, twisted shape and bracts in the form of a cross, with nail prints on each edge. This can only be legend since flowering dogwood did not grow in the Holy Land in the time of Christ.

Indians and settlers of this country used the wood for bows. Indians also boiled its bark for medicine for sick warriors, and early settlers took it for malarial fever. During the War between the States, the blockaded Confederacy used dogwood extract in place of quinine.

The dogwood tree is little known in Europe. In England the dogwood is but a poor shadow of its American relative.

The dogwood blossoms are not flowers but bracts, changed leaves, made into white to attract insects for pollination.

FLOWERING CHERRY TREES

*In these days no other ideal seems worthy of us,
Or indeed possible to us, save beauty—or call it,
if you will, the dignity of human life...*

The Mayor of Tokyo sent two thousand of the finest Japanese cherry trees to Washington, D.C., as a gift to the wife of President William Howard Taft. And so began Washington's famous Cherry Blossom festival.

This lovely Yoshimo cherry is the one most admired by visitors to Japanese temple gardens. The Kwanzan cherry, whose name means "gateway to the mountain," is perhaps the most beautiful double flowering cherry. The Okebono, "Daybreak," is a lovely, early pink flowering type of the Yoshimo cherry. There are more than ten thousand of them in the city of Tokyo.

A favorite is the autumn flowering cherry, *Prunus Subjirtella Autumnalis*, which begins flowering in October. The flowers are rather small, but they are borne in clusters and make the tree look as if it has been sprinkled with snow. The flowers open every time there is a warm spell in winter, and in spring there is a burst of bloom.

The winter blossoms are white, and the spring flowers are flushed with pale pink. Their delicate beauty is worthy of space in any garden.

GARDENIAS

Write on your hearts that every day is the best day of the year.
— *Ralph Waldo Emerson*

"Many of the elegant country house gardens have hedges of that beautiful plant, the Gardenia, mis-called in England, the Cape Jessamine," Sir Charles Lyell, the celebrated naturalist wrote of his second visit to America in 1849.

This "glory of the Southern garden," as it is called, was named for Dr. Alexander Garden, of Charleston, South Carolina, born in 1730. Linnaeus, the famous Swedish botanist, christened the plant in Garden's honor. Some authorities claim that the gardenia is native to the Cape of Good Hope.

Trailing gardenias with their delicious fragrance and exquisite blooms make a charming ground cover around boxwood and clematis.

The blossoms also lend themselves to arranging. Mrs. John Lambert for her daughter's bridal table centerpiece used a three-tiered crystal and silver epergne. In the large bottom tier, she placed beautiful, fresh gardenias, on the second tier smaller gardenias, and on the third and top tier she arranged many little trailing gardenias. The pleasing green foliage accentuated the velvety snow white beauty of the flowers.

Mr. Bob Strother, well known among gardeners for his exquisite seasonal arrangements, makes an arrangement of gardenias and the comparatively new lacecap hydrangea which is a spectacle of rare beauty.

HEMEROCALLIS

by Luther James Cooper*

"Beauty for a day" is the meaning of the Greek word, hemerocallis, and in grandma's day everyone had a clump of single or double hemerocallis where its short-lived orange flowers flourished and multiplied. Still referred to as the "ditch bank lily" it is among the garden plantings in Williamsburg and Old Salem.

Hemerocallis has been grown for centuries in both Europe and China. For almost a thousand years it has been cultivated as a vegetable in China and rated as a food delicacy. Only recently has it been used there for anything but food. It was first used for landscaping in England, and here in the United States it has been hybridized into the lovely plants that we have today.

The breathtaking modern day lily came into being in 1893 with the introduction in England of the first hybrid clone, Apricot. Florham was introduced into America in 1899. Pink Dream, the first pink day lily, was hybridized by Frank Childs in 1947 after three years of hard work in which he grew and tested more than ten thousand seedlings.

High Noon, a deep goldish yellow, large and ruffled, thick-substanced, opening at night to stay open all the next day, caused me to "fall" for day lilies. In my Raleigh garden I use day lilies for landscaping and for seasonal bloom, from the first week in May through July, with rebloom on some until frost strikes.

---

*Mr. Cooper, past president of the Men's Garden Clubs of America, and past president of the American Hemerocallis Society, has been in demand all over the country as a show judge and lecturer.

HIBISCUS
(Rose of China)

I bring fresh showers for the thirsting flowers,
From the seas and the streams;
I bear light shade for the leaves when laid
In their noonday dreams.
— *Percy Bysshe Shelley*

In the golden age of Rome the poet Virgil named a flower "hibiscus," and nothing could be gayer or lovelier than the ancient bushes of blue, red and creamy white hibiscus, with the maroon blotch on each flower.

Together with pink geraniums, blue morning glories and the orange trumpets of begonia, they ramble about the village gardens of France, even tumbling over the little balconies.

The late Dr. Clarence Poe, editor of the *Progressive Farmer* commented that "hibiscus are inexpensive, beautiful and very easy to grow." Even the African fringed hibiscus, usually a very sparse bloomer, repays any trouble when one of its splendid buds bursts open."

The Hibiscus Rose Sinensis has been grown for centuries, not only for its beauty, but because its buds are used in soups and curries. Several species native to Eastern North Carolina are often called "rose mallows."

Hibiscus Esculentus is a gift to us from Africa and is called okra or gumbo. It grows wild in the upper Nile area as well as in Ethiopia.

Thomas Jefferson said okra was growing in Virginia before 1781. During the War Between the States the ripe seeds of okra were sometimes roasted and ground as a substitute for coffee.

The hibiscus begins blooming about June 15 and blooms on into early October when the leaves die. The roots are not injured by winter and the clumps may be multiplied by subdivision. It should have fertile soil, but gardeners find no need for spraying or dusting. It thrives in soils ranging from sandy to loamy and in full sun. The flowers range in color from red to pink, salmon, white and gold tones.

HYACINTHS

*I cannot see what flowers are at my feet,
Nor what soft incense hangs upon the boughs.*
— *John Keats*

  On a cool spring morning with the sunshine bright upon them, the beauty and fragrance of hyacinths dazzle the senses. For hundreds of years Persian and Turkish rugs have been designed with these flowers. Muntham Court was called the "crown garden" because the design was taken from the crown of a baby's cap two hundred years ago.
  The earliest flower arrangement we know of is a mosaic dating from the second century A.D., recently discovered at the Quintilla Villa on the Appian Way and afterwards transported to the Vatican.
  During the peak of the hyacinth mania in Europe ten pounds was an ordinary price for a fine bulb. A single hyacinth bulb of the King of Great Britain variety sometimes sold for as much as one hundred pounds—$500.

LILACS

Every spring the lilacs bloom beside the farmhouse doors just as they did for the Jesuit fathers who grew them in Europe. We know that lilacs have long grown in the East. Ancient caravans carried the lilac from China to the gardens of Persia, and F. M. Myer, famous plant explorer who lost his life in Asia seeking new flowers, found lilacs growing wild in a faraway corner of China. Pierre Belon, a French naturalist, wrote of the flower as long ago as 1565 when the Austrian ambassador took lilac seeds from Constantinople and planted them in his garden in Vienna. In 1828 botanists discovered the lilac growing wild in the Balkan mountains. In 1905 seeds of these wild lilacs were sent to the Arnold Arboretum in Massachusetts.

The first hybrid lilac was grown in a botanical garden in France in 1777. Victor Lemoine of Nancy, France, who lived until 1911, became one of the world's greatest plant breeders, and it was he who created the beautiful modern lilac. His son, Emile Lemoine, became known as the world's greatest authority on lilacs.

Loved for its delicately scented flowers, the hybrid lilac in shades of purple, white and pinkish lavender makes a gorgeous arrangement. One arranger adds yellow roses, deep rose spray carnations, white stock, yellow gladiolus and yellow carnations to the lilacs. She first defoliates the branches and immerses them in deep water.

Mrs. N. E. Egerton, of Tatton Hall in Raleigh, has a large garden of these delicately scented flowers in shades of purple, white and pinkish lavender surrounding an informal pool.

LILY OF THE VALLEY

It's little bells hang like fair lamps of snow.

In 1568 Thomas Hyll, in the earliest book on gardening in the English language, described "the wood lilie or lilie of the valley . . . [as] a flower marvelous sweet, flourishing especially in the spring time."

Lilies of the valley have been proclaimed in religious symbolism and in poetry and art for centuries. "A Vase of Flowers in a Window," by Bosschaert (1573-1622) is a very fine flower painting which glorifies the lily of the valley as does "Vase of Flowers" by Jacop de Gheyn (1565-1629). Gutzon Borglum, the sculptor for Stone Mountain, Georgia, who lived in Raleigh for several months, once commented that lilies of the valley were greatly esteemed by Russian florists.

Mrs. Gordon Sinclair of Raleigh suggests one way to enjoy the flower's beauty. "A large silver and crystal epergne, filled to overflowing with hundreds of lilies of the valley, has a fresh, fragrant, springtime delicacy."

MAGNOLIAS

The soft leaves dangle all around me—
The wind steadily keeps up its hoarse soothing music,
Nature's mighty whisper.
— *Walt Whitman*

Although the first White House garden was planned for John Adams and landscaping began in earnest during Thomas Jefferson's administration, it was President Andrew Jackson who introduced the famous magnolias which still thrive there. These Presidents believed with Archibald Rutledge that the "great book of Nature is the First Gospel; that all one needs to enter the great gallery of living masterpieces is a willing and sensitive heart; that only in this universal Taj Mahal of God can we find peace, perfect peace."

Among the magnolias is "Glory of Winter," the Oriental magnolia. But the first to bloom is the Magnolia Stellata, or Star Magnolia, which seldom waits for winter to recede before a myriad of little white stars appears. The Star Magnolia on Raleigh's Capitol Hill, planted by George Cherry, has inspired many people to plant this exquisite, long-lasting small tree, and the Magnolia Grandiflora, with its wide, shining evergreen leaves and "carved ivory" blossoms, abounds in North Carolina.

PEONIES

The flowers sprang up in a spring song of joy
In the most wondrous wind of change
That ever swept the world.

Spring Dawn, Rising New Year's Sun, Finest Brocade, Flight of Cranes, White Moonflower, Clear Crystal White, Jewelled Lotus, Long Hedge of Camellias (a lovely double pink variety), Forever Happy, etc.—these are the enchanting names of some of the tree peonies.

Chinese literature is full of legends about the tree peony, called the king of flowers. The Chinese have been cultivating peonies for thousands of years. More than eight hundred years ago a Chinese writer told of an enthusiast who had 60,000 peony plants. Three hundred years before Christ the legends were already gathering about these flowers. The peony was taken from China to Japan by Buddhist monks and by 1890 had been introduced to the United States.

According to legend, the peony took its name from Paion, the doctor of the gods who used the milky extract of peony roots to dress the wounds of Pluto after his encounter with Hercules.

One peony plant may produce from forty to fifty magnificent flowers borne on stiff erect stems above foliage which is highly decorative. Beds of peonies in autumn can be as charming as flowering borders in spring. The leaves with their tints of gold, orange, scarlet, rose and purple brown are invaluable for flower arrangements at a time when flowers are scarce.

Some nurserymen suggest planting peonies in beds raised six inches above the adjacent earth, so as to prevent water running over the beds, which may lead to infection by nematodes.

The peony was the favorite flower of the artists Manet ("A Vase of Peonies") and Renoir ("Spring Flowers").

POINSETTIAS

Through the blue depths of the sky the bird flies,
But the tips of its wings are never stained in it.
— Paul Green

Dr. J. R. Poinsett of South Carolina, a member of Van Buren's cabinet and our first ambassador to Mexico, introduced the first poinsettia plants from Mexico into the United States in 1829. He sold a few plants to Robert Buist, a Philadelphia nurseryman, who named the flower in honor of Dr. Poinsett.

Mexicans call it "Painted Leaf," "Flower of the Holy Night," or "Fire Plant."

President and Mrs. James K. Polk visited Dr. Poinsett at his South Carolina home and were enchanted with his poinsettias. While there Mrs. Polk decided on the design for her inaugural gown. On the day of her husband's inauguration as President, the Worth-designed gown with its flaming poinsettias brocaded into yards of light blue silk, created a sensation and catapulted the poinsettia into immediate popularity in this country.

The poinsettia has firmly established itself as a Christmas potted plant, and North Carolina is considered one of the major states to produce potted poinsettias. Dormant stock plants are obtained in April for the purpose of producing vegetative cuttings, which are potted in 2¼-inch pots and rooted under mist. Upon rooting, several plants are transplanted into a larger pot. Careful manipulation of light, moisture and soil are some of the factors necessary in producing a quality plant for December.

RHODODENDRON

"Enjoy the king of all shrubs, the rhododendron, for its grandeur and delicacy and fantastic range of color," said one grower who was awed at the beauty and fragrance of the rhododendrons in the Chelsea Flower Show at the famous Rothschild gardens in England.

Rhododendrons originated millions of years ago in southeastern Asia where they are found in such wild profusion and variety that 321 species grow in one district alone. They range from tiny plants to giant trees soaring up eighty feet or more.

In 1876 about fifteen hundred hybrid rhododendrons were brought to America for the great centennial exposition at Philadelphia. Ted Van Veen, a grower from Portland, Oregon, famous for his work with rhododendrons, commented, "The gardening public began to clamor for this most beautiful flowering evergreen shrub yet seen on the eastern seaboard."

Apart from their glittering gifts of color and form, rhododendrons have another supreme merit: they require little attention. However, the successful cultivation of rhododendrons depends on the selection of sorts which can tolerate summer heat.

Rhododendrons come in colors from yellow to almost black, though pink is the favorite color. Two which bloom in March and start the season off are Pioneer and P. J. Messitt. Different varieties bloom on until August when the Polar Bear's branches are laden with scented snow.

Sir Malcolm McMillan, of Finlaystone Castle, Scotland, on a visit to our North Carolina mountains, compared the glorious rhododendrons there with the rhododendrons of his native Scotland.

SMILAX

*Flowers are the immortals that tie together
our yesterdays and todays, and link our
time with endless tomorrows.*
— Joan Dutton

The evergreen smilax is one of the most beautiful vines in the world. Generations of Southern women had used it for decoration long before there were any professional florists. Our grandmothers had it brought to the house from the swamps and streams and frequently had it planted on a trellis at one end of the porch or in some place where they could enjoy it all winter. It makes a lacy evergreen awning for a porch or outdoor living room.

Before long, the thin, pointed, glittering green leaves became popular with Northern florists, and they had it shipped North in crates for wedding decorations. Now in the South it is so rare that for you to obtain a plant, a neighbor or friend may have to divide his smilax with you. The vine grows from fifteen to twenty feet in a season. Some gardeners cut out all the dead branches twice a year. Others cut their smilax to the ground every year before the new growth starts.

Tubers of smilax are almost pure starch and were used by the Indians to make a sort of flour. All sorts of curative powers were assigned to the sarsaparilla tea which the early settlers made from different species of smilax.

In China and Japan the same ideas existed about one of the smilax vines which grew in those countries. Tons of "Chinaroot" were sold on world markets as medicinal when Japan and China were opened up for foreign trade.

The Cambridge Botanic Garden in England boasts a type of smilax from North Africa which possesses brilliant red berries.

THE COFFEE TREE

The old sheik, Abdel Kater, wrote, "Oh, coffee, thou disperseth sorrow, thou art the drink of the faithful, thou giveth health to those who labor, and enablest the good to find the truth."

In 1857 tinsmith Julius Mickey erected one of the largest coffee pots in the world to advertise his place of business in Winston-Salem, North Carolina. William McKinley risked his life to serve coffee to wounded Union soldiers on the front line at Antietam battleground. Thirty years later his comrades rewarded him by helping elect him President of the United States. On a more international scale we find the Arab belief that coffee was brought to earth by the angel Gabriel for the prophet Mahomet.

Gardeners who are interested in unusual plants have long enjoyed learning about the coffee plant. Coffee trees grow wild in Abyssinia and are cultivated in many tropical countries, from sea level to six thousand feet. Good coffee is produced in Arabia, India, Java, Malaya, Guatemala, El Salvador, Brazil, Colombia and Costa Rica. Locally, there is a very fine coffee plant located in the greenhouse of North Carolina State University. The grower of a coffee plant will find that after about five years the plant will produce a crop of "cherries," as the fruit is called. About two thousand cherries are required to produce a single pound of coffee. This is more than the annual crop of one tree. The tree's delicate white blossoms are similar to jasmine in form and fragrance.

Poet and politician John Milton said, "One sip of coffee will bathe the drooping spirits in delight beyond the bliss of dreams." Alexander Pope, who depended on the steam of hot coffee for relief from headaches, wrote, "Coffee ... makes the politician wise and [see] through all things with his half-shut eyes." Sir Francis Bacon also commented on the benefits of coffee, which "comforteth the brain and heart and helpeth digestion." London coffee houses were called Penny Universities because they were meeting places for these and other poets and philosophers. Coffee was introduced into America in 1668.

THE PERSIMMON TREE

As we bless others we feel a great lifting of the spirit, joyful, joyous, radiating health, luminous and serene.
— *T. Lichtenstein*

Dr. Clarence Poe advocated in *The Progressive Farmer* that we increase the number of persimmon trees on farms since they furnish sustenance for wildlife at a time when wildlife is so rapidly decreasing.

Poe explained that in his boyhood persimmon wood was in great demand for certain types of lumber. As a result, trees were cut and sold to such an extent that not since then have persimmons been found in such abundance.

A pitcher of persimmon beer, he said, used to give variety to the fall and winter menus on most Southern farms, and the *Progressive Farmer* carried the following recipe for persimmon pudding:

"Beat two eggs and ¼ teaspoon salt. Pour slowly over 1½ cups persimmon pulp. Mix well in a baking dish, set in a pan of warm water and bake at about 250 degrees until pudding is set."

John Charles McNeill, a former poet laureate of North Carolina offered another comment on the persimmon in his verse: "de simmon tree it natchly don't eat up de land but makes it sandbed rich."

ON BLUEBERRY HILL
WITH KATIE AND BILL McNALLY

Our blueberry hedge is eye-catching when blooming in the springtime and also in the fall when it is a mass of autumn gold. These twenty-year-old bushes have never been pruned and some are seven feet tall.

The wild birds come but do not bother the bushes as long as the feeders are kept full. We do not spray our bushes, "Tiff Blue," "Garden Blue," "Delight" and "Homebell," but remove by hand any insects which appear on them.

We enjoy eating the blueberries right off the bush, using them on cereal, in muffins, pies, cakes, dumplings and over homemade vanilla ice cream. We preserve them and freeze them—wash, drain and package.

VIOLETS AT PITY'S SAKE
Concord

One day, being weary, Orpheus sank down on a mossy bank. Where his enchanted flute fell, there bloomed the first violet.

At Pity's Sake, near Concord, the home of the late Mrs. Charles Cannon, president of the North Carolina Antiquities Society, there was an immense bed of violets. Visitors came from near and far to stand or kneel before that bed of beauty.

The late Mrs. Sprague Silver, of Midway Plantation in Raleigh, grew Parma violets. She was fascinated by the story of Napoleon gathering violets from his beloved Josephine's grave before he departed for St. Helena. These he wore in a locket until he died.

For a Christmas dinner table, Mrs. N. E. Egerton, Sr., used a centerpiece of winter roses, fragrant sweet violets, and pink perfection camellias.

MY MOUNTAIN HOME IN MAGGIE VALLEY

by Voit Gilmore

The snow had begun in the gloaming
And busily all the night
Had been heaping field and highway
With a silence deep and white.

Twenty inches of snow fell on our mile-high retreat above Maggie Valley this week, and our family shared the silent beauty of nature's white extravaganza with a number of resident grouse, boomers, deer and a lonely bluebird which seemed to have his seasons confused.

Here at the eastern edge of the Great Smoky Mountains National Park we skied or snowshoed through what the spring thaw will turn into $640,000 worth of water to be consumed this year by thirsty people and industries of the French Broad-Tennessee-Ohio-Mississippi watershed. A forester here says that an acre of forest produces $32,000 worth of water each year, going by average city water rates. The two hundred acres of hemlocks, firs, white pines and oaks here, with almost two feet of snow, appear capable of supplying more than the usual runoff in 1969.

Each season has its special wonders in high Haywood County. Even before winter snows have melted, a gay procession of wildflowers bedecks the Great Smoky Park's eight hundred square miles in a colorful parade which lasts into late autumn.

No other area in eastern America has so large a variety of plants. Botanists have found more than 1,300 kinds of flowering plants within the park, about 2,000 species of fungi, nearly 350 mosses and liverworts and 230 lichens.

From late March to mid-May there are dogwoods, laurel and flame azaleas. June brings rose purple rhododendron and the white rhododendron of June and July.

Around our mountain home nestled against the park boundary up above five thousand feet, we delight in finding columbine, trillium, gentian, May apple, monkshood, lady's slipper, sarvis, teaberry, Turk's-cap lily and pipsissewa.

In other seasons we sit in alpine sunshine watching heavy rains below. Such variations in elevation, rainfall, nature and slope of the rocks and temperature assure a variety of flowering plants and trees within the park, equivalent to a botanical motor trip from North Carolina to Canada.

Annual rainfall exceeds one hundred inches in the mountain top spruce-fir forests, while fifty inches is typical in the foothills. Mountains are often ten to twelve degrees cooler than lower areas. Such variations cause the Great Smoky Mountains National Park to boast almost as many kinds of native trees as are found in all of Europe.

As a lumberman, I have long admired the park's luxuriant hardwood coves of yellow buckeye, basswood, yellow poplar, eastern hemlock, white ash, sugar maple, yellow birch, beech, black cherry and red oak.

Specimen trees abound in the park, some even world champions in size—yellow birch fourteen feet in circumference and ninety feet tall, a yellow buckeye sixteen feet around and eighty-five feet high, and an eastern hemlock twenty feet around and ninety-eight feet high.

NORTH CAROLINA TREES IN HISTORY AND IN LEGEND

by C. C. Crittenden*

North Carolina has its full share of famous trees. The stories connected with them rest upon mere legend rather than upon reliable historical evidence, but this fact need not detract in the slightest from their romantic appeal. Indeed, if anything, the lack of certain knowledge serves to enhance their romance and charm.

Roanoke Island

The Eagle Nest Pine represents the first English colony in the New World. The settlers sent out during the reign of Queen Elizabeth I by Sir Walter Raleigh, a favorite of the queen, came to Roanoke Island. There Eleanor Dare, wife of Ananias Dare, gave birth to a daughter, Virginia, the first child born of English parents in the New World.

The settlement mysteriously disappeared, and today we know it as the Lost Colony. When John White, governor of the colony and grandfather of Virginia Dare, returned after several years absence, he found the settlers gone and the word "Croatan" carved on a post and the letter "C" cut on a tree, indicating supposedly that they had gone to live with the Croatan Indians, who made their home nearby.

What their fate was we will probably never know, but today there stands at the edge of Fort Raleigh an old tree, known as the Eagle Nest Pine, which is said to be the very tree on which the letter "C" was cut.

New Bern

Just off Chance Street, on the banks of the Neuse River in New Bern, is a very old cypress under which the first vessel built in North Carolina is said to have been constructed and launched, under which the early colonists are reputed to have signed treaties with the Indians, under which General Nathaniel Greene and other notables are reported to have made speeches, and

*This article first appeared in 1938.

under which George Washington and others are said to have rested.

Hertford

In the town of Hertford are two cypress trees under which William Edmundson and George Foxx, both members of the Society of Friends, are declared to have held the first religious services in North Carolina.

Oriental

Teach's Oak, in the town of Oriental takes us back to the days of the notorious pirate, Blackbeard, or [Edward] Teach. Treasure is rumored to have been buried beneath the roots, and the ground all around reputedly has been dug up by treasure hunters.

Catawba County

On the Robinson Plantation in Catawba County is an oak which stood at the home place of Henry Weidner, thought to have been the first white settler in the area. The story is told that once when Weidner and his family were driven away by the Indians an understanding was made with a friendly redskin to keep one side of the tree painted red as long as it was dangerous for them to return, and that is the way the family escaped harm.

Guilford College

Standing in the graveyard of the Old Friends Meeting House is the Liberty or Revolutionary Oak, under which are said to be buried twenty soldiers of the Revolution. The spot is marked by a tablet.

Wilkesboro

Here is the famous Tory Oak on which Colonel Benjamin Cleveland is said to have had five Tories hanged.

Greensboro

Guilford Battleground near Greensboro boasts two famous trees. There is the Battleground Oak, to which General Greene is thought to have tied his horse during his important battle with Cornwallis. The twisted top of the tree today is said to prove that the horse ate out the top of what was then merely a sapling.

A fine old persimmon tree, two and a half feet in diameter, stands on the very spot where Lord Cornwallis reportedly had a gray horse shot from under him.

Wilmington

The Washington Oak is on North Carolina Highway 30, fifteen miles east of Wilmington. Here [George Washington] is said to have rested his horse on his southern tour of 1791. Its branches arch over the highway and nearby is a tablet placed by the DAR.

Chapel Hill

Here is the Davie Poplar. In 1792 William Richardson Davie, father of the University of North Carolina, is said to have sat under it while he wrote his description of the site chosen for the University. Nearby is a small poplar, rooted from the original, which will become known as the Davie Poplar when the parent tree is no more.

Raleigh

In the northern part of Raleigh is the well-known Henry Clay Oak. Under its branches in 1844 reputedly sat the dashing Clay when he wrote his far-reaching "Raleigh" letter, opposing the annexation of Texas, and perhaps costing him the presidency for which he was a candidate.

Monroe

Near N. C. Highway 200, seven miles southwest of Monroe, is

the Richardson Oak. It is said that Edward Richardson, Revolutionary hero, was about to be hanged from this tree by sixteen Tories when he was rescued by a band of Whigs summoned by his young wife. Tradition adds that the Tories were then lined up and shot by their former prisoner. It is said that they were buried in one grave.

These and many other famous and beautiful old trees stand within the borders of North Carolina. Each has its own past and each its own story to tell. We can but wish that the voice of the wind as it sighs through their moss-grown boughs could speak our language and tell us what happened underneath in years gone by.

NORTH CAROLINA PARKS

by Paul Kelly

Flanked on both its western and eastern boundaries by two great national parks and having numerous state parks, historic sites and other outstanding scenic, recreational and historic attractions between its borders, North Carolina truly upholds its reputation as "Variety Vacationland."

Most popular of all National parks, the Great Smoky Mountain National Park, encompassing some 514,093 acres, straddles the North Carolina-Tennessee border with about half in each state.

The report of a committee of experts in this field, recommending the Great Smokies as a national park in 1924 after months spent in studying and investigating the southern mountain region, fittingly described the area so: "of [the] possible sites the Great Smoky Mountains easily stands first, because of the height of the mountains, depths of the valleys, ruggedness of the area and the unexampled variety of trees, shrubs and plants."

At the other extremity of North Carolina, some five hundred miles away, a scenic and recreational attraction of entirely different type is Cape Hatteras National Seashore. In fact, it differed so radically from the established national parks, a new category, "Seashore," was created by Congress to describe it.

This reservation includes some seventy miles of the barrier reefs known as "the banks," separating the Atlantic Ocean from the sounds. It is one of the few remaining undeveloped stretches of beach in the country, and although man can use its many recreational and scenic facilities, it is to remain as nearly as possible unaltered and unspoiled.

Another national seashore, Cape Lookout, extends along "the banks" a distance of some fifty-eight miles from its beginning at Ocracoke Inlet to Beaufort Inlet.

Between these great national reservations, the state has created a widely dispersed and varied system of twenty-four state parks and two nature preserves with a wide variety of recreational, scenic and historic features. Some of the units are new and are undergoing development. The number of users runs into the millions each year.

The Division of State Parks of the Department of Natural and Industrial Resources is working toward a goal of twenty acres of parkland per one thousand population in North Carolina.

First among the state parks was Mt. Mitchell, which has the distinction of being the highest peak in the United States east of the Mississippi River, its summit reaching 6,684 feet above sea level. The nucleus of the park was purchased with a special appropriation of $20,000 by the 1915 General Assembly. Its purchase was viewed as somewhat of an emergency by Governor Lock Craig and others, as lumbermen had begun to remove the timber.

Through subsequent purchases, the area of the park has reached 1,469 acres. From a thirty-eight-foot observation tower atop the summit, a magnificent panorama stretches over a vast area of mountains and forests.

In 1924 Fort Macon was turned over to the state by act of Congress. The ancient fort constitutes the major attraction of the park. It is notable for fine detail and excellent workmanship.

Construction was started on the fort in 1826 and was completed in 1834. Cost was approximately $463,700. With its moat, casements, graceful arches and thick walls, the fort is considered one of the most important historical relics in the State. Its location at Beaufort Inlet near Atlantic Beach makes it easily accessible and one of the most popular state parks.

A decade passed after the acquisition of Fort Macon before any new units were added. In 1935 three new state parks were established—Morrow Mountain, Hanging Rock and Cape Hatteras. The latter was first a state park but was deeded to the Federal Government in December 1952 for inclusion in the Cape Hatteras National Seashore.

Beginning with the mid-thirties, the latter half of the decade showed the greatest expansion in the system experienced in a similar period up to that date, with seven units added.

The program was greatly stimulated as a result of development facilities furnished through various Federal work relief agencies, more particularly the Civilian Conservation Corps Camps. There had been no State appropriation for capital improvements up to that time, the first being $500,000 in 1947.

Camps consisting of two-hundred-man units were established in virtually all of the parks, most of them operating for several years. These camps brought new life to the state park program. Their activities included forest fire fighting, fire control measures, erecting fire towers, establishing water systems, building roads, building bath houses and swimming pools and making other capital improvements.

As a result of this and other emergency programs, the State was saved millions of dollars. This work contributed materially towards making the parks more useable and popular with the public.

Currently (1976) there are twenty-six state parks, including several established in the last few years, and two nature preserves. Several of these areas are now under development and not in general use.

To meet their goal of twenty acres of park land for each one thousand population, the State Parks Division must acquire almost double the present acreage by 1980.

In the years following the establishment of the first state park (Mt. Mitchell), the administration of state parks was under the direction of the state forester. J. S. Holmes, the first state forester, was a pioneer in state park development and an outstanding champion of an adequate park system.

In 1935 Thomas W. Morse became the first full-time administrative state park official. Morse became chief of a newly created state parks section of the Division of Forestry under state forester Holmes. He supervised much of the spending of Federal Emergency funds.

Following Morse's retirement, Thomas C. Ellis became the chief executive of the division, with the title of Superintendent of state parks, a position he still holds.

During recent years the pace of state park acquisitions has quickened. Former Secretary of the Department of Natural and Economic Resources, James E. Harrington, was quoted in 1974 as saying that North Carolina had acquired more state park acreage in the previous fifteen months than it had in the fifty-six year period from 1916 to 1972.

This acquisition amounted to 32,885 acres and was used for the development of new parks in seven areas and for major additions to four existing parks.

As the state's park system has expanded there has been an increase in use of the parks. In 1949 the total attendance at the state parks was recorded as 746,867. The next year attendance grew by almost 50% to 1,116,746. In 1965 the figure was 2,092,519. In 1972 attendance at state parks was pushing three million.

Originally sites of historical significance were included in the state parks system. However, the General Assembly of 1955 directed that areas in this category be turned over to the Department of Archives and History. These were the Town Creek Indian Mound, Montgomery County; Battle of Alamance State Historical park, Alamance County; Old Brunswick Town, Brunswick County; James Iredell House, Edenton, Chowan County; and the Charles B. Aycock birthplace, Wayne County.

The four national forests in North Carolina—Pisgah, Nantahala, Croatan, and Uwharrie—with a total area of 1,129,000 acres, have set aside a number of areas for public recreation, including camping, hunting, fishing, hiking and other public uses.

Popular publicly owned scenic and recreational areas in the state include the Blue Ridge Parkway, said to be America's most scenic parkway; Kerr Reservoir, a multipurpose project of the U. S. Army Corps of Engineers, much of which is open to the public; and the new Cape Lookout National Seashore.

These are the North Carolina state parks:

Boone's Cave — 110 acres, Davidson County. About fourteen miles west of Lexington. Reported to be the place where Daniel Boone spent much time.

Carolina Beach — 441 acres, New Hanover County. One mile from Carolina Beach. A "naturalist's delight" with Venus' fly-trap, a botanical wonder endemic to the area. Family camping.

Cliffs of the Neuse — 572 acres, Wayne County. Fourteen miles southeast of Goldsboro. Summer naturalist on duty. Year-round family camping. Limited youth wilderness camping.

Crowder's Mountain — 421 acres in Gaston County. Seven miles southwest of Gastonia.

Dismal Swamp Land — 14,400 acres, Camden County, north of Elizabeth City. Crossed by old canals of historic significance. Atlantic white cedar exists in one of the last remaining stands.

Duke Power — 1,328 acres, Iredell County. Campsites.

Eno River — 1,200 acres, Orange County. 3½ miles west of Durham.

Fort Macon — 385 acres in Carteret County. Restored historic fort, museum, bathing beach.

Goose Creek — 1,300 acres on Pamlico River southeast of Washington, North Carolina.

Hammocks Beach — 892 acres on Bear Island, Onslow County. Three miles of ocean front, said to be one of the most beautiful and unspoiled on the Atlantic Coast. Free passenger ferry service Memorial Day to Labor Day.

Hanging Rock — 4,040 acres in Stokes County. Vacation cabins. Campsites.

Jockey's Ridge — 300 acres at Nags Head in Dare County. Encompasses largest natural sand dune on the eastern coast, which ranks among the highest in the world.

Jones Lake — 1,893 acres, in Bladen County. Campsites.

Modoc Mountain — 2,300 acres of rolling topography in Halifax County. Rough camping.

Merchant's Millpond — 1,800 acres in Gates County. One of the state's rarest ecological communities. Cypress swamp with large pond.

Morrow Mountain — 4,425 acres in Stanley County. Vacation cabins. Campsites. Museum.

Mount Jefferson — 539 acres in Ashe County. About one mile west of Jefferson, near the Blue Ridge Parkway.

Mount Mitchell — 1,469 acres in Yancey County. Eastern America's highest peak topped by observation tower. Restaurant (seasonal), museum, recreation lodge, and tent campsites (None for trailers).

Pettigrew — 17,369 acres (including 16,600 acre Lake Phelps) in Washington and Tyrrell Counties. Historical structures. Rental boats. Campsites.

Pilot Mountain — 3,635 acres in two sections in Surry and Yadkin Counties, connected by unique 5¼ mile corridor for hiking and horseback riding. Large quartzite monadnock resin, 1,500 feet above countryside.

Raven Rock — 2,700 acres, six miles northwest of Lillington in Harnett County. Unique plantlife. Scenic and historic area. Rough camping.

(Theodore) Roosevelt Natural Area — 250 acres in Carteret

County. Rare coastal zone flora. Marine Science Research Center, not yet open for public use.

Singletary Lake (Group Camp) — 1,221 acres in Bladen County. Twelve miles southeast of Elizabethtown. Headquarters for eight state lakes.

Stone Mountain — 2,109 acres in Wilkes and Allegheny Counties. Seven miles west of Roaring Gap. 600-foot-high granite pluton, three miles around at base.

William B. Umstead — 5,214 acres in Wake County. Two sections, Crabtree and Reedy Creek. Eighteen miles of bridle trails. Campsites. Swimming facilities, rental boats.

Weymouth Woods-Sandhills Nature Preserve — 425 acres, one mile east of Southern Pines. Long leaf pines. Museum.

WILDFLOWERS OF NORTH CAROLINA

by Dr. B. W. Wells

> *"Of the plants growing in this country, I have given an Account of not the hundredth Part of what remains; a Catalog of which would be a Work of many years, and more than the Age of one Man to perfect, or bring into regular classes, this Country being so very large and different in its situation and its Soil."*

So wrote the early naturalist John Brickell, in eastern North Carolina in 1737. In this work we find the key to the floral wealth of the state—great diversity of soil and climate. The exquisite purple oxalis or mountain wood sorrel (*Oxalis acetosella*), a common wild flower of Canada, is in North Carolina joined geographically to the equally attractive starflower (*Pleea tenuifolia*), which comes into the state from Florida.

Between these extremes are to be found nearly five hundred genera of wildflowers represented by approximately eighteen hundred species, a fact which has made North Carolina famous as a botanical collecting ground and as a source region for innumerable species introduced into gardening.

The highland flowers of the eastern United States reach their maximum development in kind and number in the North Carolina mountains. The rarest of all the mountain wildflowers, Shortia, has never been found outside the state.

The fresh water marshes present an astounding array of attractive flowers which because of inaccessibility are poorly known. For the great display we must look to the flat, wet savannas. On these grassy, boglike areas the wildflowers grow with an abandon seen nowhere else and on many of the areas such as the Big Savannah of Pender County, the flowers grow in such profusion as to rival our cultivated gardens. The Big Savannah is the largest and finest natural wildflower garden in the eastern United States. Abundant flowers are available for any type of garden—rock or bog, sun or shade, clay or sand.

The Woman's Club of Raleigh, 1979

Unfortunately, only a handful of the many people who helped make North Carolina and her flowers and gardens as beautiful as they are today could be mentioned in the preceding pages. Here we offer a tribute to many of these other gardeners of North Carolina.

PAST PRESIDENTS OF THE GARDEN CLUBS OF NORTH CAROLINA

Miss Edna Maslin — Winston-Salem	1925-1927
Mrs. R. D. Gapen — Reidsville	1927-1929
Mrs. S. B. Halstead — High Point	1929-1931
Mrs. John B. Cramer — Wilmington	1931-1933
Mrs. Wesley Taylor — Greensboro	1933-1935
Mrs. H. R. Totten — Chapel Hill	1935-1937
Mrs. R. L. McMillan — Raleigh	1937-1939
Mrs. J. Buren Sidbury — Wilmington	1939-1941
Mrs. D. J. Lybrook — Advance	1941-1943
Mrs. Robert T. Cecil — Asheville	1943-1945
Mrs. J. S. Mitchener — Raleigh	1945-1947
Mrs. Fred J. Bartlett — High Point	1947-1949
Mrs. James Tyler — Kinston	1949-1951
Mrs. Roy M. Homewood — Chapel Hill	1951-1953
Mrs. E. A. Palmgren — Charlotte	1953-1955
Mrs. George W. Little — Lilesville	1955-1957
Miss Louise Ballard — Waynesville	1957-1959
Mrs. J. B. A. Daughtridge — Rocky Mount	1959-1961
Mrs. P. Frank Haigler — Monroe	1961-1963
Mrs. Roscoe D. McMillan — Red Springs	1963-1965
Mrs. W. C. Landolina — Winston-Salem	1965-1967
Mrs. L. Barron Mills — Laurinburg	1967-1969
Mrs. John M. Reichard — Raleigh	1969-1971
Mrs. W. Marion Odom — Ahoskie	1971-1973
Mrs. J. Ross Pringle — Greensboro	1973-1975
Mrs. L. Phil Wicker — Greensboro	1975-1977
Mrs. Gream Yates — Charlotte	1977-1979

PAST PRESIDENTS OF THE NORTH CAROLINA FEDERATION OF WOMEN'S CLUBS

Lucy Bramlet Patterson — Winston-Salem	1902-1905
Lillian Watson Alderman — Henderson	1905-1907
Margaret Lovell Gibson — Wilmington	1907-1909
Laura Holmes Reilley — Charlotte	1909-1911
Sallie Southall Cotten — "Cottendale," Bruce	1911-1913
Adelaide L. Fries — Winston-Salem	1913-1915
Clara Souther Lingle — Davidson	1915-1917
Kate Burr Johnson — Raleigh	1917-1918
Ida McDonald Hook — Charlotte	1919-1921
Mary Lou Jackson Cooper — Henderson	1921-1923
Cornelia Petty Jarman — Raleigh	1923-1925
Gertrude Sills McKee — Sylva	1925-1927
Annie Land O'Berry — Goldsboro	1927-1929
Marie Long Land — Statesville	1929-1931
Lucille Hassell Hobgood — Farmville	1931-1933
Mamie Brown Latham — Durham	1933-1935
Nancy Miller Marshall — Mount Airy	1935-1937
Ethel Godfrey Etheridge — Hertford	1937-1939
Lewellyn Williams Robinson — Wallace	1939-1941
Katie MacAulay Rankin — Mount Gilead	1941-1943
Kate Herring Highsmith — Raleigh	1943-1945
Frances Farrell Bishopric — Eden	1945-1947
Blanche Gaskill Gupton — Charlotte	1947-1949
Stella Williams Anderson — West Jefferson	1949-1951
Maude Davis Bunn — Raleigh	1951-1953
Jewel Sumner Kirkman — Greensboro	1953-1954
Dorothy Heath Brown — Greensboro	1954-1956
Katharine Shenk Mauney — Kings Mountain	1956-1958
Mary Cross Dent — Raleigh	1958-1960
Mabel Claire Maddrey — Raleigh	1960-1062
Margaret Taylor Harper — Southport	1962-1964
Evelyn Sherrill Bunch — Statesville	1964-1966
Marjorie Yates Yokley — Mount Airy	1966-1967
Norma Phaup Cates — Faison	1967-1968
Juanita Martin Bryant — Boonville	1968-1970
Eleanor Smith Keller — Smithfield	1970-1972
Elaine M. Odenwald — Greensboro	1972-1974
Minnie Lou Creech — Tarboro	1974-1976
Mollie Johnson — Thomasville	1976-1978
Peggy Moffett — Charlotte	1978-1980

PAST PRESIDENTS OF THE WOMAN'S CLUB OF RALEIGH

Miss Fannie E. S. Heck	1904-1907
Mrs. W. S. Primrose	1907-1909
Mrs. T. Palmer Jerman	1909-1911
Mrs. T. P. Harrison	1911-1913
Dr. E. D. Dixon-Carroll	1913-1915
Mrs. Clarence A. Johnson	1915-1917
Mrs. George W. Lay	1917-1918
Mrs. J. R. Chamberlin	1918-1919
Mrs. B. H. Griffin	1919-1921
Mrs. W. T. Bost	1921-1923
Mrs. Josephus Daniels	1923-1925
Mrs. R. Y. McPherson	1925-1927
Mrs. F. R. Perdue	1927
Mrs. T. E. Browne	1927-1929
Mrs. J. W. Bunn	1929-1931
Mrs. Clarence A. Shore	1931-1933
Mrs. E. L. Layfield	1933-1935
Mrs. John Vincent Higham	1935-1937
Mrs. J. S. Mitchener	1937-1939
Mrs. Charles G. Doak	1939-1941
Mrs. J. Henry Highsmith	1941-1943
Mrs. Robert M. Cornick	1943-1945
Mrs. R. L. McMillan	1945-1947
Mrs. R. N. Simms	1947-1949
Mrs. Josephus Daniels, Jr.	1949-1951
Mrs. Leslie B. Evans	1951-1953
Mrs. L. Y. Ballentine	1953-1955
Mrs. Earl W. Brian	1955-1957
Mrs. Harold J. Dudley	1957-1959
Mrs. Maxwell Warlick	1959-1961
Mrs. David C. Worth	1961-1963
Mrs. Bern F. Bullard	1963-1965
Mrs. Leif Valand	1965-1967
Mrs. James A. Odom	1967-1969
Mrs. Kern Holoman	1969-1971
Mrs. C. Gordon Maddrey	1971-1975
Mrs. W. Guy Mendenhall	1975-1977
Mrs. R. Paul Bullard	1977-1979
Mrs. A. C. Broughton, Jr.	1979-1981

PAST PRESIDENTS OF
THE RALEIGH GARDEN CLUB

Mrs. C. A. Shore	1925-1926
Miss Isabell B. Busbee	1926-1927
Mrs. L. A. Mahler	1927-1929
Mrs. H. C. Evans	1929-1930
Miss May V. Johnson	1930-1932
Mrs. R. N. Simms	1932-1934
Mrs. R. L. McMillan	1934-1936
Mrs. Perrin Gower	1936-1938
Mrs. R. Y. McPherson	1938-1940
Mrs. A. Wray White	1940-1942
Mrs. Marion F. Wyatt	1942-1944
Mrs. J. Wilbur Bunn	1944-1946
Mrs. Walter B. Willard	1946-1948
Mrs. R. O. Caveness	1948-1950
Mrs. L. R. Harrill	1950-1952
Mrs. Graham B. Egerton	1952-1954
Mrs. T. W. Ruffin	1954-1956
Mrs. Walter A. Watts	1956-1958
Mrs. R. A. Isley	1958-1960
Mrs. J. Emmett Pollock	1960-1962
Mrs. Edith Crane	1962-1964
Mrs. John D. Minter	1964-1966
Mrs. Milton Abbott	1966-1967
Mrs. Clyde P. Patton	1967-1968
Mrs. David M. Wood	1968-1970
Mrs. Marvin Johnson	1970-1972
Mrs. Gerald Erdahl	1972-1974
Mrs. John L. Troutman	1974-1976
Mrs. Elaine Callas	1976-1978
Mrs. William Finch Troxler	1978-1980

PAST PRESIDENTS OF
THE WAKE COUNTY MEN'S GARDEN CLUBS

Glenn Randall	1947
Dr. T. T. Spence	1948
Robert Schmidt	1949
W. N. H. Jones	1950
R. L. Cope	1951
N. M. Wiser	1952
R. S. Dunham	1953
Graham B. Egerton	1954
M. E. Gardner	1955
Col. W. S. Brier	1956
Dr. Fred Cochran	1957
Dr. J. B. Gartner	1958
Col. W. W. Brier	1959
Dr. S. T. Walton	1960
Henry Maddux	1961
Franklin Correll	1962
A. H. Veazey	1963
H. K. Witherspoon	1964
W. G. Avent	1965
W. Howard Norman	1966
Louis A. Horis	1967
C. L. Haney	1968
Luther J. Cooper	1969-1971
John Hornbuckle	1972-1973
Dr. Frank Poole	1974-1975
Guy Mendenhall	1976-1977
O. D. Fleming, Jr.	1978-1979

PAST PRESIDENTS OF THE RALEIGH ROSE SOCIETY

Mrs. Marion Wyatt
Mr. R. W. Shoffner
Mr. Glenn O. Randall
Mr. J. C. Richert, Jr.
Mr. R. H. Pearce
Dr. J. S. Rhodes
Mrs. Sam Ragan
Mr. Russell G. Broadus
Mr. E. J. Anderson

Mrs. C. L. Norton
Mr. B. Moore Parker
Mr. Howard Hicks
Mr. Floyd Lutz
Mr. A. L. Haskins, Jr.
Mrs. Cuyler Poore
Mr. Aston Perry
Mr. Henry Rasor
Mrs. D. W. Tierney

PAST PRESIDENTS OF THE NORTH CAROLINA CAMELLIA SOCIETY

Mrs. R. L. McMillan — *Organizing Chairman*
Duncan DeVane — Fayetteville
Robert Holmes — Mount Olive
David Rose — Goldsboro
W. P. Kemp — Goldsboro
Henry Rehder — Wilmington
Clay Foreman — Elizabeth City
David Oates — Fayetteville
Dr. Ed Vaughan — Greensboro
Junius Powell — Whiteville
George C. Hampton, Jr. — Greensboro
Larry L. Trammel — Chapel Hill
Irvin Nixon — Elizabeth City
George Ross — Wilmington
Tom Clark — Clarkton
Fred G. Hahn, Jr. — Charlotte
George Herndon — Fayetteville
Marshall H. Rhyne — Belmont
Ernest Aycock — Smithfield
William S. Howell — Wilmington

The North Carolina Governor's Mansion.

OUR FIRST LADIES

Our governors and first ladies have been a great inspiration to many gardeners. They have loved flowers and encouraged their cultivation across North Carolina. The state has been fortunate in the gracious women who have been our First Ladies. They have tried in every way possible to grow and cultivate and also to encourage North Carolina's gardeners.

Dr. Ellen Winston presents the following tribute to every first lady who has been hostess in the Governor's Mansion during the term of office of each elected president of the Garden Club of North Carolina.

How shall we honor whom we revere —
Lover of all the arts and of our land?
How, but to cherish Beauty's every flower:
How, but to live with Beauty, and so be
Apostles of Rejoicing to mankind?
— *Mary Lee McMillan*
North Carolina Clubwoman
March 1942

MRS. A. W. MCLEAN — 1925-1929

Thoughtful and generous, Mrs. McLean was an elegant hostess for many organizations and groups. She was noted for the beautiful arrangements of flowers in the Governor's Mansion and for the excellent cuisine. Not overly strong, she nonetheless carried out her duties with grace and charm.

MRS. O. MAX GARDNER — 1929-1933

Beautiful and stately describe Mrs. O. Max Gardener, who maintained the high standards of her predecessor in presiding over the Governor's Mansion. While giving pleasure to others through numerous social functions, she invariably expressed her appreciation of their presence on such occasions.

MRS. J. C. B. EHRINGHAUS — 1933-1937

Youthful and lovely, Mrs. Ehringhaus overcame the restrictions of the Depression years to maintain the Governor's Mansion as the focus for many delightful social affairs. One of her special interests, which has flowered over the years to the joy of the citizens and the renown of the state, was the North Carolina Art Society.

MRS. CLYDE R. HOEY — 1937-1941

Acclaimed by all who were privileged to know her for her friendliness and hospitality, Mrs. Hoey had deep compassion for the unfortunate. She believed in the rehabilitation of prisoners. Through her efforts the prison greenhouses became a major source of flowers for the Governor's Mansion and still is to this very day.

MRS. J. MELVILLE BROUGHTON — 1941-1944

Thoughtful and kind to all, Mrs. Broughton opened the doors of the Governor's Mansion wide not only to innumerable groups within the community and state but also to thousands of service men from the military installations of World War II. At the same time she began the arduous task of refurbishing the Mansion. A unique tradition had its beginning when the Raleigh Garden Club decorated the Mansion at Christmas in 1944 with the public invited to enjoy the holiday atmosphere.

MRS. GREGG CHERRY — 1945-1948

Gracious but retiring, Mrs. Cherry continued to make the Governor's Mansion a center of hospitality and support for a great variety of organizations. Again the Raleigh Garden Club took responsibility for the exquisite Christmas decorations. Mrs. Cherry was especially interested in music. She brought many splendid musicians to the Mansion, adding this much appreciated facet to the entertainment of groups, large and small.

MRS. W. KERR SCOTT — 1949-1952

"Miss Mary," known throughout the state, was gentle and unselfish. She met her obligations fully and unassumingly while maintaining close ties with ongoing activities at the farm in Haw River. As in prior administrations the Governor's Mansion was opened for innumerable social functions, presided over by this quiet, gracious, kindly First Lady.

MRS. WILLIAM B. UMSTEAD — 1953

While her tenure as First Lady of the State was brief due to the serious illness and untimely death of Governor Umstead, Mrs. Umstead carried her heavy burdens with patience and dignity. Unable to participate in the usual schedule of public functions at the Governor's Mansion, she was ever thoughtful and gracious in her private relationships.

MRS. LUTHER HODGES — 1954-1960

Handsome and poised, Mrs. Hodges presided over the Governor's Mansion for seven years. She entertained for countless persons from within the state and from the nation and abroad. Interested in everyone, she remained unassuming in manners and thoughtful in her concern for her guests. One of her special interests was improvements to maintain an always fresh appearance of the much-used Mansion.

MRS. TERRY SANFORD — 1961-1964

Younger than her predecessors, Mrs. Sanford brought youthful enthusiasm to her duties as First Lady and to the Governor's wide-ranging interests. Her friendliness and efficiency, her pride in "showing" the Mansion, gave an especial warmth to the social life of Governor Sanford's administration.

MRS. DAN K. MOORE — 1965-1968

The artistic talents of Mrs. Moore were immediately brought to bear on the interior of the Governor's Mansion. She sought through the most skilled advice and help available to make the furnishings and decorations as near perfection as possible. Her focus on art and beauty continue to bring rich rewards to citizens throughout the state.

MRS. ROBERT W. SCOTT — 1969-1972

Mrs. Scott again brought the attractiveness of youth and a young family to the Governor's Mansion. Busy as she was, the public hospitality never suffered. Her innate friendliness and her ability to adjust to the demands of her position made the many social affairs both cordial and relaxed. Continuing the concern for the total appearance of the Governor's Mansion, the handsome brick wall and iron gates were added during Governor Scott's administration.

MRS. JAMES E. HOLSHOUSER, JR. — 1973-1976

Another youthful mistress of the Governor's Mansion, Mrs. Holshouser presided over a busy round of social activities. Her personal interest in such areas as volunteerism and the Bicentennial celebration have been important in their development. Without complaint she spent many months in a substitute home while the Mansion was being modernized for safety and comfort and then guided the restoration of the interior to the equal in beauty of any past period.

MRS. JAMES B. HUNT — 1977-1980

Although one of the younger First Ladies of North Carolina in recent decades, Carolyn Hunt, wife of Governor James B. Hunt, has met her many and heavy responsibilities with dignity and graciousness. She shares actively in the special interests of the Governor with respect to education and to the needs of the handicapped.

Mrs. Hunt has opened the Mansion to thousands of visitors and entertained on an extensive scale. Yet she has been able to maintain a warm and homelike atmosphere for the Hunt children. She combines her official duties and family obligations with both modesty and charm.